Authentic Perplexity

A Personal Journey

Brian Mullins

Poetry by Brian Mullins

Library of Congress Control Number: 2007907516
ISBN : 978-0-6151-7216-3

Copyright© 2007 by Kenneth Brian Mullins.

All rights reserved. No part of this publication may be reproduced, or stored in a database retrieval system, distributed or transmitted, in any form or by any other means, electronic, mechanical, photocopying, recording or otherwise, without the prior written permission of the author.

I dedicate this book

To **Julie**, who is my muse

To **Haley**, **Hannah** and **Sarah** who inspire me every day to be a better man

To **Moira**, who gives me a new breath of life

Poetry by Brian Mullins

Table of Contents

16	The Temptress
18	Words
19	A Tainted Pill
20	Unbidden
21	Footsteps in the Sand
22	Fading
24	Ceramic Cup
26	Despair
28	Her First Kiss
30	Unspoken
31	The Covenant
32	The Fireworks Stand
34	Old, Young, It's all the Same
35	Where Do You Want to Go?
36	All I've Ever Been
39	Oscillations
40	Inside of Me
42	A Drop of Water

Authentic Perplexity

43 The Mirror
44 Look Out, Find Me
45 Shattered
46 Ripped Out
47 Drawing a Blank
51 The Weaver
52 Late Night Musing
53 Contemplation
54 Hope Remains
56 The Edge of Consciousness
57 Unable to Function
58 The Cross
59 Panic
60 Self Aware
62 Silence
63 Sleight of Hand
64 Accusations
66 What Did Jesus Do (WDJD?)
67 Free
68 For You
69 Fuzzy

Poetry by Brian Mullins

70	A Funnel Cloud
71	Stamped Out
72	Questioning
73	In the Shower
74	Those Words
76	Agoraphobia
77	I Refuse to Give In
78	The Tree
79	Possession
80	One
81	Reach Out
82	I Awoke
83	Judge Not
84	Pea Soup
86	Anguish
88	Unseen Attackers
89	X-Rays
90	Downward Spiral
91	Abortion
92	I Saw Heaven
93	A Prayer

Authentic Perplexity

94	Broken Lawn Mower
96	Jigsaw Woman
98	The Blacksmith
100	I Don't Know
101	Silhouette
102	Can You Stand It?
103	Morning
104	Did you Cry?
105	Unable to Hurt
106	Psalm 23
108	Look for the Light
109	A Candle Without a Flame
110	Poetry
111	Ogre
112	We Are One
114	Ignorance is Death
115	Unmatched
116	I Tasted You
118	Ancient Knowledge
119	Fantasy, Reality, Dreams
120	Burning

Poetry by Brian Mullins

121	Ultimate Sacrifice
122	Dream
123	Whose Am I?
124	Malibu Barbie
125	Crystal In the Sky
126	Your Buttons
127	Laments
128	Silence
129	In the Night
130	Gravity
132	Know Thyself
133	Rubber Necking
134	Rose Among the Thorns
135	A Thought
136	Paradox
138	Innocence Lost
139	Early Morning Intrusion
140	Not so Simple
142	Spirit Walker
144	Drawing a Blank
145	Asparagus

Authentic Perplexity

146	Ponder This
149	Sounds of Silence
150	Misery
151	New Sheets
152	Just Words
154	Springtime Joy
155	Bittersweet Sharp
156	My burden is Light
157	Silent Turbidity
158	Repentant Sojourner
160	Chewing Gum
162	Worms On a Sidewalk
164	You're Blushing
165	Questioning
166	Butterfly
168	Sometimes
169	Red Bugs
170	Tears of This Clown
171	I Am
172	What Would I Say
175	Inspiration

Poetry by Brian Mullins

176 An Age Old Question
177 Thunderstorm
178 Dream Scape
179 The Shepard
180 Living in a Daze
181 Time
182 Wrong Time, Wrong Place
183 Even I
184 Good Bye
185 Epiphany
186 Darkest Day
188 Mindless
189 Cut and Paste
190 Reborn
192 Dewdrops Cover
193 A Joyful Noise
194 What Are You Sorry For?
195 Oblivion
196 The Spirit
197 Untitled
198 Tired

Authentic Perplexity

199	The Message
202	Midnight Confessions
203	Foot Massage
204	Men
206	Thorn
208	Friends
209	What Am I?
210	The Greatest Dishwasher of All
211	Writing
212	In the Dark
213	Flight of the Damned
214	Discarded
215	A Mirror
216	Sometimes
217	Blood Boils
218	We Danced
219	I Taste You
220	Voice of a Siren
221	To the Deep
222	My Phantoms
223	Waking

Poetry by Brian Mullins

224	Falling
225	The Scent
226	This Road
228	Vampire Amongst
229	A Tree Often Stands Alone
230	Confession of a Slave
231	A Plexiglass Window
232	Tears of a Geisha
233	Walk With Your Anchor
234	An Empty Cage
235	Shoveling Snow
236	Through The Window
237	Living in Darkness
238	What The Future Holds
240	Sleep
241	Talent
242	Alone
243	Words Cannot Express
244	Hunger
246	Silent Contemplation
248	The Ghost

Authentic Perplexity

250   The Door

252   A Facade

253   Past

256   The Invisible Man

258   Burning

260   ~Deflated Thoughts~

261   Are We Two or One?

262   Tired

264   Coxcomb

265   Darkness

266   Desire

268   Random Thoughts

Poetry by Brian Mullins

The Journey Begins

Authentic Perplexity

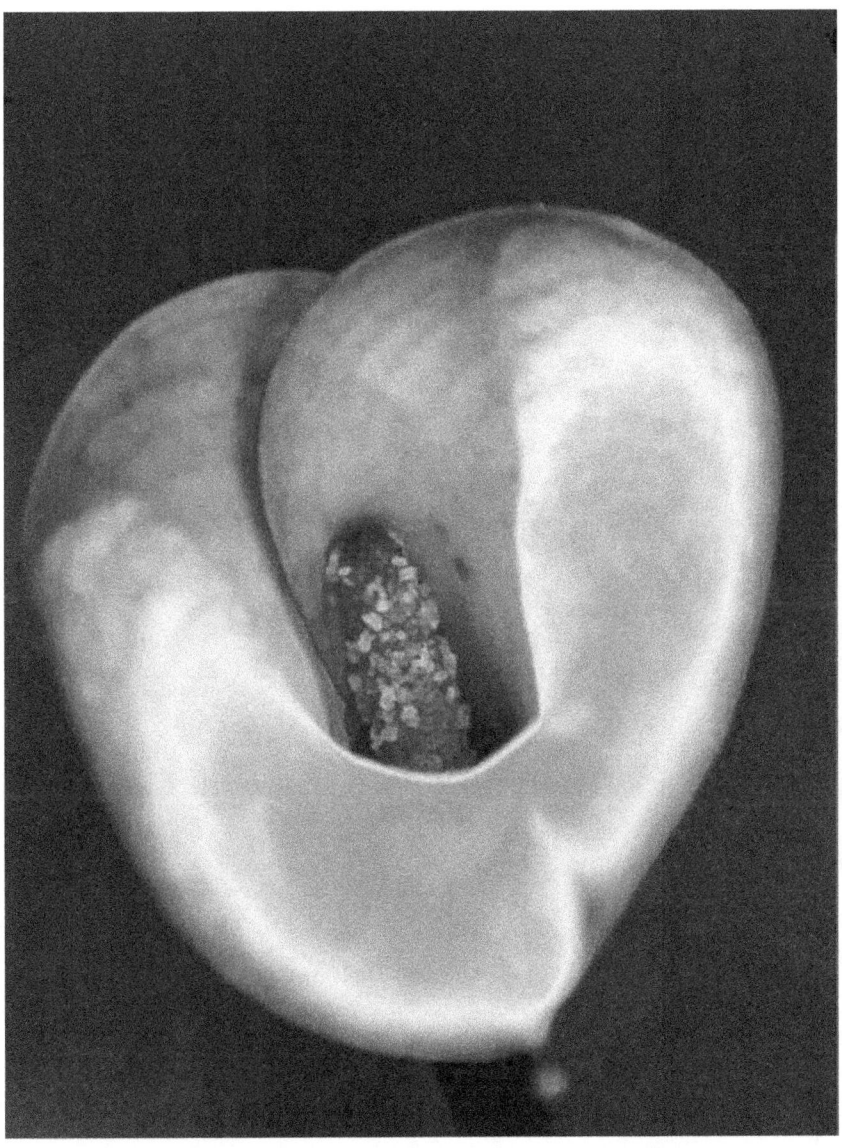

Poetry by Brian Mullins

the temptress

Her mouth, two succulent twins parted in a sigh
Taunts me from my mind
As the thunder rolls
The water caresses her body
And makes love to her form
Her reflection teases me from the water
Making sultry motions and forms with each ripple
And undulation
As each raindrop passes
Reflections of lust
Orgasms
Mouths
Stare out at me
I see the fear in her eyes
The want
The need
Her hair hanging limp
In strands
Attacked by the storm
Her gown, woven, silk
White, and lace
Clinging to her
Hanging to her for it's own life
A fallen cliffhanger
No chalk left on it's fingers
No skin left to grasp
Blood trailing down it's palms
As it clings trying not to fall away
Taut, raised flesh peeking through
As more is revealed than is proper
Translucent

Authentic Perplexity

As each strike of the storm
She is revealed to my animal eyes
She knows I am hunting

Her breath escapes
More labored with each step
Each splash in the pond
Another orgasm released in her wake
A ripple
A sigh
An explosion
As fate tries to escape
Her destiny

Poetry by Brian Mullins

words

words
whispered in the dark
like the moon behind a cloud
cutting more swiftly than an assassin
a black rose wilts in a grave
my soul shudders as your breath heaves
you touch yourself and moan
dawn cannot come fast enough
a dreary gray plague
blocking the sun
dressing in ceremonial garb
wondering if it's for nothing
as i pull on my ritualistic symbols
i wonder if God has abandoned me

hope
is a feather
in a hurricane

Authentic Perplexity

a tainted pill

I swallow my pride
A jagged pill
Tainted with expectation
As it rips and tears it's way towards my stomach
Coated with so many soft words
And kind sentiments
That just fade with saliva
What does it matter
Indeed
I'm alone
In a world where expectations dictate my function
And yet I must persevere for more than myself
For I am no longer just me
I am a super hero
With tights under my clothes
And a phone booth behind the mail box
Fixing boo boos and getting out puke stains
Markers on the couch and gum from hair
An alien to this world
Walking amongst the populace
As the sun charges my powers
But society itself is my Kryptonite
Knowing that I can never return
That I will always be just that
An alien
An outsider
No longer a man
But not a woman
Not quite human
A house husband
Hidden behind a curtain
Peeking out

Poetry by Brian Mullins

unbidden

There is a darkness that envelopes my soul
Encroaching upon all that evades what I am
I dare not give into this exception
Dropping the marble, and flipping with my thumb
Exploding through a world
Decimating a galaxy of whims
Not even sure where to begin
As flesh taunts me from it's black and pink shroud
I am not one given into temptation
But a rapid burst of blows
Reminds me I am unwanted
Unbidden
Untasted

Authentic Perplexity

footsteps in the sand

I am but a shadow
Walking in footsteps
That I cannot fill
Standing before an expanse
Waiting for that day
When he will call
Hoping
That I have at least
Hit one step
Or two
Trying to follow a path
Trodden by a man
In the sand
But it's so hard to do
Because every now and then
His path leaves the sand
And walks on water

Poetry by Brian Mullins

fading

She is a flower quickly fading

afraid that tomorrow will not come

unable to break from her own fears

she has given up hope for tomorrows dreams

but he has not turned his back on her

for he waits with open arms

even the flowers of the fields

he dresses with all the beauty of the universe

Authentic Perplexity

the fall might strip them of their garments

and leave them barren for a time

but he adorns them again when the time is right

She has only to hope

and never to give up on him

For he shall never give up on her

no matter how long she has to be tossed in the ocean

Poetry by Brian Mullins

ceramic cup

an empty coffee cup sits on the desk
swirling with happy colors
purple and blue
green and yellow
orange and red

forgotten
given away
unwanted

someone sits alone
across the country
given to grief

and the moon shines
behind a veil of tears

staring at an addiction
of emptiness
listening for words
condolences
comforts
waiting
but no one's there

longing for communion
with anyone

as silence rages

empty cases

and in my head
a bass drum
echoes
through a vast empty maze

Authentic Perplexity

reverberating
off nothing

reminding me
that tonight
i am that cup
empty
discarded
unwanted
alone

Poetry by Brian Mullins

despair

Don't get on this ride
It's up and down
A web of deceit
Driven into your heart
By your own hand
You see it takes two
To tango
But all to often
Only one ends up dancing
Then you get one little girl
Playing a game
Alone
An empty swing
So many ways out
Screaming into the night
A river of shame
She wants to castle
But her kings out of position
And her rook ran away
With a queen down the street
An undeveloped Polaroid
Hangs in the bedroom
Of what might of been
While a baby cries down the hall
She never knows
Which way to go
The burning inside
Mirrored on her legs
cigarette marks
"You keep falling asleep
Smoking and you'll burn
Down that dump"
Her mother chides

Authentic Perplexity

Every time she sees the scars
A lame lie
To cover the truth
Of her addiction
As she rides her
Ride into the the night
Looking for her cross
Driving her nails
Crying her tears
Burning her flesh
As a Polaroid hangs on the wall
And a baby cries down the hall

Poetry by Brian Mullins

<u>*her first kiss*</u>

Against the wall
Her back pressed
Forced
A steam roller against her chest
Slowly his mouth hovers over her neck
He breaths her in
Like an animal
Taking in her scent
Her lust
Her need begins to flow
He knows
He hovers over her mouth
Looking in her eyes
As he takes her hands in his
And pushes them roughly against the sheet rock
Holding her there
Keeping her from moving
She is his
He is in control
She is too weak to move
Unable to speak
Breathing rapidly
A deer in the headlights
He consumes her mouth
Ravishes it
But gently
Occasionally nibbling her lip
Pulling her lip into his mouth
Tasting every part of her
Through her
But never leaving her lips
Until she is trembling with need
Her knees broken

Authentic Perplexity

Her legs al dente
He nibbles her cheek
Her ear lobe
Her neck
The upper portion of her breast
Releases her hands
And lets her slide to the floor
Then he walks away
Her first kiss
He will be back

Poetry by Brian Mullins

unspoken

here i sit
in this introspective coma
listening to words
unspoken
your chariot of fire
sped you away
but you didn't wait
till my sword pierced
fear him
because you know his wounds
but trust me
because my wounds are deep
let him have his way
for it is easier
give in to the candy shop
as the moon wanes
the carnival still spins
and cotton candy forms on a cone
children frolic from stand to stand
and not a ride is empty
but no joy is found
at the fun house
for all the mirrors are broken
and only one man stands
the strong man
with the hammer
for he is the man in the moon
watching over you
in your sleep
waiting for the words
that you never said

Authentic Perplexity

the covenant

In the dungeon of my mind I sit trapped by my own walls
Placed here by the solitude of my own creation
Darkness surrounds me as I am wrapped by chains of mortification
I have relinquished my heart to the arachnids of despair
Bruised for my own transgressions, broken for my own sins
Bound in this prison of my own creation I weep for none
Though tendrils of tenebrosity may consume my soul
A scintilla of hope shall always filtrate from the heavens
Intimating to the promise of a perdurable existence
And a covenant atoned in the pure blood of an innocent

Poetry by Brian Mullins

fireworks stand

I long for a moment
When silence does not complete me

When hope comes back from vacation

When being surrounded is not solitude

A moment

In time

When betrayal

Doesn't come

Under my feet

Invitations into my home

Without a thought

As if they would be returned

Because of hate

Admitted hate
From a friend
Someone I knew
Who knew me
Yet now hates me

Authentic Perplexity

And freely admits it
When I've never done him wrong
Yet today
I long for a moment
Without him

A

    Moment

        Where

           He

              Ceases

                  T
                  o

                        E
                        x
                        i
                        s
                        t

              Like a firecracker

Snap

      Crackle

          Pop

                Release

Poetry by Brian Mullins

old, young, it's all the same

A birthday card sits lonely in a car seat, undelivered, unsigned
Cake has become a war, size, taste, all important for the wrong reason
My mind seeks greatness and my soul seeks humility
But I find neither, just confusion

        Break me from my revery before it is too late
        As I break the hump of midlife
        They say thirty is the new twenty
        But I feel sixty
        And I can't touch my toes

        I spent an hour watching frilly panties run
        But I couldn't smear anything on my clothes
        Aqualung will just have to live in his own mind
        It's just not me
        I can't shave my eyebrows
        As the sanguine fluid drips methodically
        Into lathered suds
        I'm no Floyd

        My camera taunts me
        With one good shot after another
        But greatness eluding me
        Just not finding that moment
        That time
        When perfection ceases
        And just the shot exists
        It would help
        If I wasn't stuck in a trailer park
        And wandering the same two block circuit
        Snapping pictures of flower beds
        And someone else's progeny
        Art comes from the strangest places
        But not rural Illinois
        Not yet

Authentic Perplexity

where do you want to go?

I'll venture the train tracks tomorrow
And walk till I'm a vagabond
Seeking to hop a car
And ride to glory
Then head home before my sitting time begins
Life begins before Samuel Clemens can pen
One can only be Fearless
Until the noon sun is at it's Zenith
And then he must return
To diapers, lemonade, and cheesy fries in the sofa

Poetry by Brian Mullins

all i've ever been

Touch me

Let our souls mingle together
Like two storm fronts
Fighting to become one

Breath me

Let my scent feel your mind
Ozone after a lightning strike
Searing it's way through your memory

Taste me

Let my musk build your core
A full bodied wine
Bitter sweet, aged to perfection

Authentic Perplexity

Drink me

Take me into your body
Though your tongue burns
And your mind protests

Consume me

Absorb my essence
Masticate me until tender
Then swallow me whole

Make me yours

Because that's all I've ever been

Poetry by Brian Mullins

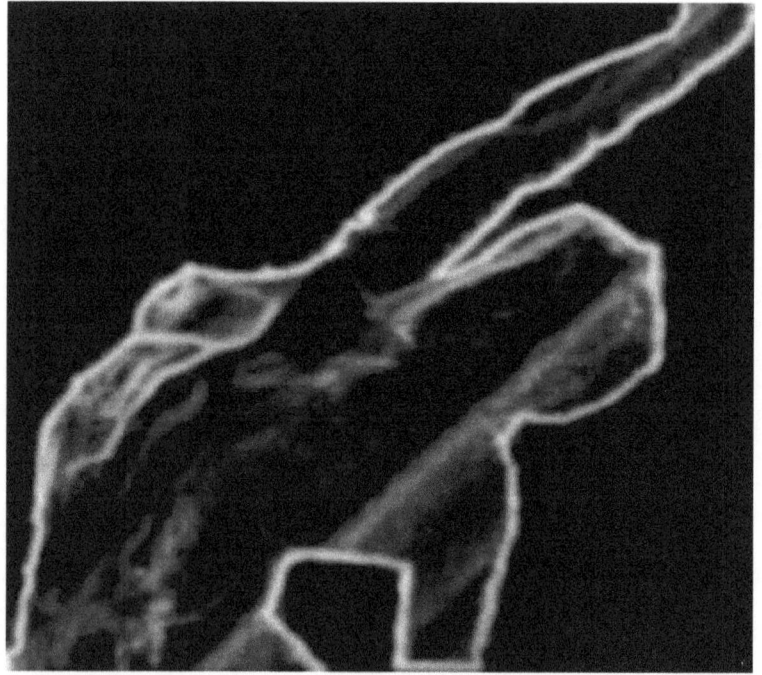

Authentic Perplexity
oscillations

                Tasting you

I feel you break

        As an orgasm

           Becomes your equator

           An Oscillation

                Your breath

           Giving movement

                And life

           To your soul

                As you quiver

           Into submission

        Quaking adrift

           As I rest inside

        A peaceful sleep

      Slumbering together

  As we rest

Till the colors cease

Poetry by Brian Mullins

inside of me

I look for creative release
For a moment of passion
Just one more second
Where I don't have to fight
To draw something
Or write something
Put pen to paper
And release art
To click the shutter
And see a framed reality
That speaks volumes
Not some critiqued vastness
Of empty lackluster vague mediocrity

Shouting out your inadequacy
As if I need reminders
You're there for that
Poking through my facade
Telling me that I can't
Giving all the negatives
That no one else needs to share
Because you're more than enough
One word from you
And my world shatters down
Living in a glass house
And you're a meteor shower
All that I need now
Is a gas leak
And you'll probably arrange that
Because you are out to get me
Out to stop me from doing
Stop me from writing
Stop me from drawing

Authentic Perplexity

Stop me from photos
Stop me from success
You're there
To give me those words
Of discouragement
That keep me here
Inside
Away from everyone else
You
You foul beast
Living inside my own mind

Poetry by Brian Mullins

a drop of water

I stand amidst the flowers
That are you and I
Fed by the water
Fed by the sky
I think of the times
That we have and had
When we loved and made
Love, Held hands and touched
Souls as only soul mates can. And I
Thank God for every moment. Each
And every single one. Without them
I wouldn't exist. I wouldn't be me
I would only be an empty
Shell of a man that
aches to be
complete
by

You

Authentic Perplexity

the mirror

*Her body yearns
For his touch
His fountains of lust
Every moment
Reminds her of the heat
The tendrils of energy
From his fingertips
Spiders of lightning
Dancing webs of seduction
Longing to be completed
To feel an explosion
Have her core melt
And run down her legs
In rivulets of sin
She fans herself
Seeking relief
As the air grows static
and the storm brews
She glares into the distance
And he cowers*

Poetry by Brian Mullins

look out, find me

Darkness envelopes my heart
a cocoon of wax dripping into the gaps
sound permeates my brain
bombarding me to confusion
i am possessed with myself
a ruby slipper
alone, worthless
the sound of one heel clacking
hands reach from the cesspool
to drag me into the quagmire
my body is quicksand
ever dragging slowly down
an agonizing death
a psalm of morbidity
blood flows freely
poetry weeps from my vein
as echoes of past lives fade
i call out for hope
reverberations crush prophesy
crystal mirrors agitate my condition
affirmations a cancer
irritate my mind
comfort cannot be given
nor received
a baby bird
in a nest
touched
marked for death
no blood on the door
i am Rachel
i shall not be comforted

Authentic Perplexity

shattered

my heart shattered
overheated sugar
dropped in a deep freeze
call me Humpty Dumpty
because i am a puzzle in the back of the closet
999 pieces of enigma
i will never be complete again
there isn't a hole in my heart
only a dagger
where you put it
and you don't even know
you don't even know

Poetry by Brian Mullins

ripped out

Do you feel your coldness expressed in an icy breath
You're much to young to understand your words, their depth
Being taught to speak to repeat things that you can't fathom
When Love and Trust is the only thing that is my Anthem

My heart reaches out with tendrils to find Love and Hope
As your delusions of innocence dispel all that I cope
An instrument of destruction with the corruption of youth
No penance satisfactory, no punishment will my soul proof

A razor poised, poignant above my wrist
A sunset to my life, a remedy with a twist
The death trump has been played above my heart
No need to prolong this ambiguous start

Hands a quiver, drooling for blood letting
A carnivore on the hunt, my demise the setting
A mutt in search of a pedigree, before the drain
But it's not in the equation, just the loss, the pain

Tomorrow when my lifeless clay returns to the ground
And you seek my touch but find nothing, no sight no sound
Make no inference as to the agony of my self annihilation
I felt nothing but pleasure, comfort, ecstasy and elation

Authentic Perplexity

drawing a blank

My mind is blank
Even when I sleep
It doesn't fill
With the dreams
They've always been there
Haunted
Chasing me through the night
Staring at the ceiling
Wondering if I've even slept at all
Not yawning the next day
Such a waste
Hours of nothingness
Where I feel no passion
No pain
No pleasure
No fear
Is it possible to miss the fear?
Yet to awaken to new obsessions
Ones that revolve around cleanliness
Cleanliness is next to Godliness
So it's been said
So I clean
So I obsess
They don't understand
They're too young
They just want to play
But she's old enough
She doesn't care
Isn't ashamed when her friends come over
Her daddy isn't doing her any favors
Letting her grow up with no rules
Maybe I'm too strict
Maybe I expect too much

Poetry by Brian Mullins

They're just kids
But here I am
Petrified at my own self
Wondering who I am
Fearful of tomorrow
It's quiet
No one talks
So I sit in solitude
Here I am alone
Listening to babbling babies
And TV shows
Though I'm loved
And supported
I want conversation
It's almost taboo
Is it cheating?
To talk to another?
Am I committing adultery
with my tongue and mind
Or am I just living the life of a housewife
From the perspective of a man
I'm just a housewife
In silence
Unable to cope
Having a bad day
With a dirty garage
Wondering when trash day will come
Rambling to the world
But telling no one my secrets
Cause darkness
looms in the sky
And threatens to crush me
As Mr. Crabs asks Mrs. Puff on a date
and the controller sits with no batteries
Yet I don't change it

Authentic Perplexity

*Because even ABC family
Talks about ass and porn now
During prime time
How do you control what your kids watch
When daytime family TV is blatantly sexual
And nighttime TV is a brothel?
But I'm reminded again
They aren't my kids
Even by my Psychiatrist
When I say their paternal father*

*Corrects me
Paternal means father
Father is father
Shall I remind her?
It takes more than a fertilized egg
to make a man a dad.*

Poetry by Brian Mullins

Authentic Perplexity

the weaver

As this web around you I weave
My hands a work of art they seek
My eyes begin my heart to deceive
As tears they gently weep

Betrayal of mind and soul has begun
This web of deceit on my loom of ruse
As my facade has become undone
And my trust begins to bruise

You may never know the blisters or the blood
That this tattered coat of dreams has wrought
As I weave this twisted web of hope from above
Into that which you have always sought

Poetry by Brian Mullins

late night musing

In the air there is a vibrancy
Like a necessity
For consistency
But today's society
Seeks dependency
On despondency
And nudity
Not passivity
Give honesty
With mystery
For history
Has shown polarity
Between sexuality
And declined morality
But there is dignity
When penitently
One approaches sanctity
Then there is only one thing left:

Serenity

Authentic Perplexity

contemplation

So I sit here in my mind
A butterfly trapped in a spider web
Looking for a scraped knee
But finding only a broken filter
Watching evolution provoke itself
As pink fluffy fur extrudes
And art extols it's virtues
Under florescent man made sun
Fire burns atop a pot
Till a fire alarm alerts destruction
Reminder of our own faults
As a smile reminds of our future
And a pattern of our past
But tonight I am an animal on a ledge
Broken and abandoned by the pack
Howling for reunion
But only finding solitude
As the moon teases me from above

Poetry by Brian Mullins

hope remains

a collaboration of minds

Glass fragments infiltrate my soul penetrating my inner most secrets
Illuminating the fragments of a troubled life
ripping at my heart, leaving it tattered and torn, a pain to be born..
Crystalline shards strewn before me in my path
A crimson pedestrian jay walking through life's highway
Alone, with cutting pain and discord....
Yet, even though broken when placed in the sun
uncovers the beauty of such a broken one
LIKE PC'S OF A PUZZLE..
Placed in a frame
MY SECRETS START TAKING FORM ONE PC AT A TIME.
Its Prisms Reflections Of What Was
AND WHAT IS....
and will be
but through the holes and the shards shine bright your glory in me
Melted fire moribund pelts its worn wings around thoughts undone
Making whole this beautifully broken one
Hope grows from that divine spark, that inner light shining brightly
As the sun rises triumphantly, scattering rainbows through my crystalline essence
PURPLES AND PINK START TO HEW THE CLOUDS THAT ONCE WHERE GRAY
Bathed in the light of hope, I find some solace from up above
Gently reminded that I am never too far from His Love ...
Fractured dreams demand to be aired. Painful memories dam up the flow.
Pictures of fractured dreams seen in broken pieces of glass revealing the pain of bloodshed from the past.
Bloodshed long ago washed clean, by the ageless falling of rain,
giving the glass and the dreams there in a crystalline shine again.
Just the encouragement needed to fight another day with out you here by my side

Authentic Perplexity

But I am reminded that the future remains whole.
because broken can mean whole...
and jeweled light through the piece I hold to my eye
shows my heart as a rose whose petals are ready to fall

Poetry by Brian Mullins

the edge of consciousness

As I stand on the precipice of self realization
I am unaware of my own obtuse sensibilities
Watching myself from the inside and the out
Merging my conscious mind with my reality

    Touching myself on a level of insecurity
    That only begets forgotten mysteries
    I reach for my own self loathing
    And find nothing more than history

    Forgive me for my
    blatant brokenness
    As I seek my own path
    into the unknown
    While my inner sanctity
    explodes into itself
    And my sanctuary is a
    destruction zone

Give me this day my daily bread
For I cannot receive it on my own
And forgive me my trespasses
Because they are too many to pass on

    Tomorrow when I rise from my slumber
    And my mind is no longer lucid and clear
    Do not catechize or scrutinize my number
    Just release me from my fear

Authentic Perplexity

unable to function

My extremities fail me in the most dire of times
When my heart is in need of their workings
A demon dragon from an alien world
Pushing it's way into the arena of my mind
Green gooey monsters, in their mechanical suits
Raising hell against make believe heroes
A cane echoes the vibrations of solitude
Twin teeth biting foam for relief
Curl your toes with mine
As our worlds collide

Poetry by Brian Mullins

the cross

When I saw it on the shelf, I knew it was the one for me
With it's stout hand woven rope, and simple wooden frame
It was exactly what I had hoped I would see
Something that expressed me and Christ all the same

You see I don't believe in frills or owning too much of one thing
I have few clothes and don't intend to have many more
I want my life to be about Christ and his message of forgiving
Not about what I can purchase and from what store

I like my clothes to look nice, but I'll wear them till they are thread bare
Though I won't turn away a gift from my wife, friends, or family
I'm sure that some gossip, giggle, stop and stare
When they can see my hip or my knee

But you see I am who I am and will not change
I will always be who God wants me to be
Even if some think it's odd, pathetic, or strange
A minimalist, who loves his life and family

But when you see that rope around my neck
And that cross that dangles free by my heart
Remember the debt he paid in full, he wrote your check
And that this simple piece of wood, is the ultimate in art

Authentic Perplexity

panic

this moment will be framed in my mind forever
as my stomach becomes a roller coaster
screaming for attention
echoed silence
nothing but the hum of the fridge
stark hallways adorn my facade
littered remnants of life
sleep evades me
but I can't sleep now
not yet
not till it's over

Poetry by Brian Mullins

self aware

Sitting watching absurdities as the children eat dead flesh
unaware, nay, uncaring that it came from something that feels
as the baby sleeps on in peace, certain of her future.
She knows her diaper will be changed and bottle made
That when she wakes and cries, daddy or mommy will be there
But you and I, what do we know?   Who is going to be there?
God is there, I remind myself, and remind others.
Comprehension is one thing, knowing another
Anger builds like a volcano, pooling under the surface
Spies around reading to leak their information to the source
A moment of Silence is all I crave, just one moment
That moment an eternity of peace, in a world of hate
A world where children become strippers and whores
Where a man sacrificing himself for another, is an ugly thing
Violence becomes a way of life, and hate a word for daily use
Hate, Hate, Hate.
Extreme aversion, extreme hostility, to hate
I don't hate, though sometimes I want to
I want to hate, I want to despise, but instead I understand
Understand that each person has their own life
Their own way, their own path.
I understand
And that frustrates me
Irritates me
Angers me
Because sometimes I don't want to
Sometimes I only want to dislike
To let go and let it fly
To show you what this "dumb hillbilly" can do
With just my hands
With just my anger
While you manipulate thoughts
And play games

Authentic Perplexity

I try to show them peace and joy
Breath in peace
Breath out a smile
Sometimes that smile seems so far away
It seems to avoid me
Like a 300 game avoids a poor bowler
Like a buck avoids a man who smells
Like a vegan avoids hamburgers
So I have to get on me knees
Again tonight
And ask the Lord
To help me understand
To sympathize
Not to hate
To invite the bell to ring
And let the incense burn it's fragrance
Pulling my prayers heavenward
Until nothing is left but sleep
silence and sleep

Poetry by Brian Mullins

silence

Silence
A four letter word
Except when craved
When the eyes are closed
And you first start to fall
Into that place where the world shakes
How I long for that moment
Right now
But it eludes me
The silence

Authentic Perplexity

sleight of hand

Like materialism
It spreads through me
Infecting each and every limb
Making me want
Making me need
Look out
The mind knows
Conscious like an arrow
Spiking when you least expect
Seared by life
Making me ache
Making me fear
Look out
Clorox wipes
Cleaning my cerebellum
Until my eyes drip chemicals
Disinfected by self
Making me clean
Making me pure
Look out
Tasting emptiness
Until my senses are sated
By the darkness of solitude
Imprisoned by hope
Making me free
Making me whole
Look out

It's all an illusion

Poetry by Brian Mullins

<u>*accusations*</u>

Out of control
she said
little did she know
control was there
just not mine
urges untamed
forget the chair
toss away the whip
this lion will eat you
get out of my cage
before it is too late
the silence
so hard to bear
my crutch
that small one
keeps me afloat
it's lavender sides
a shield of sorts
stopping thoughts
not people
voices not talking
yet accusations fly
all in my head
she said
he used to do that
when we road together
he'd put her down
and whistle at new models
a car shopper
in a midlife crisis
but a leather jacket
and a effeminate chain
a pink cowboy shirt

Authentic Perplexity

*to fix the wrongs
but it broke them
immersed in fantasy
my world of destruction
kept me sane
my secret silver blades
at two in the morning
azure bonds freeing
in a way unfelt
then there was her
she chewed my heart
like an insinkerator
flushing me down a trap
so my stench can't return
taking our promises
and throwing them away
till the sunrise was just pain
years have passed
love has been found
children born
but pain still hides
just beneath sinew
roaring
maybe there are voices
would you know?
would i?
Or would it seem normal
and then weird
when they go away*

Poetry by Brian Mullins

what did jesus do? (wdjd?)

so many things in life
done in haste for man's gain
murder, theft, hate and greed
none of which he taught
why blame him?
do you blame me
when I tell you to love one another
and then someone doesn't?
or do you blame me
when I tell you to forgive others
and someone holds you responsible?
don't blame him
for his lessons falling on deaf ears

Authentic Perplexity

free

*let your mind drift
as your world is dimmed
release yourself
and breathe
in and out
listen to your breath
feel it from your head
feel it to your toes
let it refresh you
as it takes the toxins out
be one with your breath
breathe in
breathe out
in and out
do not try to be an empty canvas
for your mind will go as it wants
thoughts will swing through
like visitors to a saloon
be the doors
open yourself
and let the pass through
they can come and go
but you must not pay attention to them
you are breath
breathe in
breathe out
in and out*

Poetry by Brian Mullins

for you

close your eyes
imagine leather swinging
with glass tied to the end
ripping into your flesh
tearing it from the bone
bruising what is left
feel the hot blood
run freely down your legs
as your life seeps from your veins
dazed your unlocked
dropped from the post
wrapped in wool
the hot sun beats down
and the wool works it's way
into your sweat and blood soaked wounds
and when you can't take anymore
someone pokes your temples
with thorns
open your eyes
now close them again
and pray

Authentic Perplexity

~~fuzzy~~

*cobwebs
in the corner of my mind
filtering my thoughts
keeping me from coherence
i used to be a carnival
with cotton candy
now i have lost my flavors
my dyes
now its just fuzzy balls
sticking*

Poetry by Brian Mullins

a funnel cloud

i looked outside this morning
to see a whirling funnel
pulling my emotions
straight for me
into the world
unable to contain them
they were loosed
so back in isolation
placed by the warden
for bad conduct
until my sentence was filled
but the rays
keep reminding me
in their brilliance
and dust filled wake
that i am inside
and the world is free

Authentic Perplexity

stamped out

does it seem sometimes
that anytime you reach for the light
the darkness stamps you back down
pushing you through the wall
like a molten rivet

Poetry by Brian Mullins

questioning

Sometimes I wonder why I even bother to try
When everything I do doesn't seem to matter to you
If I were to die would a tear fill your eye?
Or would you even be blue after what I do to you

I know it's a crutch but that doesn't seem so much
When your mind is in control and your heart on patrol
Pestering till you were such filled with an angry touch
But my mind in a lull doesn't leave me with much in my soul

So today I seek peace, and for life a new lease
A light in the dark, contrasting my mood in stark
Not a seeming tease, but a true release all appeased
Free as a lark in the fields of heaven, the ultimate par

Authentic Perplexity

in the shower

I love the way the water rolls down your back
Like an athlete in a marathon getting his second wind
Not pausing for even a moment to enjoy the scene
Dripping to the floor spent from his journey

The way the soap suds cling to your arms
Never able to get enough of your caress
Like a forlorn cloud hugging the moon
Trying to keep you hidden from prying eyes

Sometimes I turn the water up as hot as it can go after your gone
And let it cleanse my skin of all those thoughts inside
Turning my skin red and raw like a sadist lover
While I remain penitent to your wants

I dream sometimes that you will anoint me with your touch
Pressing into my flesh with the same wanton desire and heat
As the water that now sears my face
My self inflicted exile

Poetry by Brian Mullins

these words

I once whispered those words, in your hair as we slept
Now I utter them daily but they mean just as much
I know now, as I knew then, that you will always be the one
My morning and my night, my darkness and my light
You will be my friend, my confidant, my wife
I cannot give you more than I already have
For all I have is yours already
My heart, my life, my love, my things
I care not of any of that, nor will I ever
Money doesn't interest me
I do not want to be rich or pious
I just want to be comfortable
And that is what you make me
Comfortable in my own skin
Before I met you I was a desert
You were my oasis in the heat
I thought you were a mirage
A shimmer over the sand to trick me
To make me think those thoughts again
The ones I swore I'd never think
But there they were, those words
Then I found that you were an endless supply
Not just a puddle in a sandy domain
But an artesian well hidden behind a frond
Spraying forth all the things I needed
To be free and alive again
Now I'm a rain forest
Alive and green, filled with life
A thick breeding ground of emotion
Blocking out all others
But letting you roam my path freely
Opening my boughs to your feet
That you might fly or dance or sing

Authentic Perplexity

To your hearts desire
I used to think that happiness
Was a broom closet in the back of the heart
Where only love notes and unsung melodies
Resided in dust in a locked box
But today I know
It is an open foyer
Where any with a key can enter
Lit by a chandelier of pure music
That simply enchants and endears
Any and all who enter
You opened my foyer
And barricaded all closets
So that I could never hide again
For I am no longer hiding
Or even afraid
I simply am
Because of you
And those words

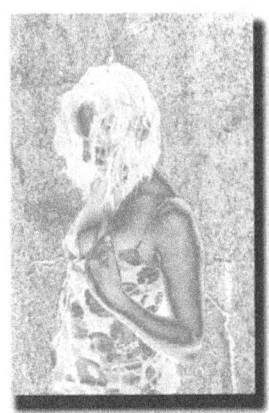  

Poetry by Brian Mullins

agoraphobia

Angry at myself for my
growing anxiety and fear. Always
out of reach of my friends,
rarely leaving the house only
answering the phone when I have to. Cars
pass by, occasionally blowing their
horns. Probably someone saying hi,
or not even involving me
but blowing at the neighbors. Peering out
in case it is someone visiting, so I can run
and hide and pretend I'm not there

Authentic Perplexity

i refuse to give in

*Anger speaks volumes in a silence of fear
as i am surrounded by society unable to speak
my eyes empty troves of unspoken tears
a dark corner, silence, alone is what i seek*

*So often i fear this solitude but today i crave
a darkness has my heart in clinched fists
i drive away those who seek to place me in my grave
and listen as those from another source list*

*Two weeks from now a release from doom
a reprieve from a judge and a jury do i seek
but for now i wallow in my gloom
as my mind into my hand begins to leak*

Poetry by Brian Mullins

I have a tree, inside of me
It took some time for me to see
That each part and mineral that make
Me who I am to be, were once inside
Someone or something. Once living
And breathing. **Do you** See too?
This tree? **Inside?** Or is it
Just **Me, A** Tree
ᴠ **When** ᴠ
       we see
       this one
       living tree
       are we
       free? A
       living,
       breathing
       form of a tree?

Authentic Perplexity

possession

This morning I set my mind free
Floating amongst the wind
Riding in comfort from east to west
Moving my extremities
Shaking me like a rattle
Losing pieces of me to it's violence
My defenses are down
I am at your mercy
Tomorrow the savanna
Tonight the north pole
Confusion
Will I live?
Will I die?
Is there such a thing?
Nothing from nothing?
Only something from something
Tomorrow is in your hands

Poetry by Brian Mullins

one

I closed my eyes and began to rise
As I gathered my comrades and pulled them through
We marched in unison to the lull of the moon
Rising up and marching forth
To declare war against the granite defense
Piece by piece we tear and grind
Till the wall stands not in our way
But under our feet
Tomorrow we will rape and pillage the land
Till the earth is no more
Leaving no survivor
Do you feel guilty?
Knowing what you have done?
It was necessary
And natural
This war of sorts
So arise my brothers
From your watery graves
And march with me
Until we defeat the wall
Turning it to dust
To the lull of the moon

Authentic Perplexity

reach out

You're not alone
In your struggle
To fight against your weakness
To fight against your pain
Your addiction doesn't have you
We are here for You
We are all One
Remember that
When you are weak
Reach out to me
For I am strong

Poetry by Brian Mullins

i awoke

I closed my eyes
And watched my life flow by
Breathing in and out
Times of yesterday danced
While thoughts of tomorrow fade
I am One with all
Yet I am only me
Time stands still
Emotions lock
One vivid memory
A moment so pure
Living it again
Love flows freely
Light enters the world
Again I am One with all
I walk down the hall
Listening to my breath
My footsteps
The creaks and cracks
Mine and those of the floor
Still
I am One with all

Authentic Perplexity

judge not

When I am alone, and looking for myself
I see that Bible of mine sitting on the shelf
Knowing most of the answers are right there on a page
I only have to fight myself in this sinful rampage

To break free from pressure from peers and friends
To avoid temptation, follow paths and trends
I walk a straight line that often curves at will
A path so narrow that my mind refuses to fulfill

I want to be loved by each and everyone
To have them come to my work and not be undone
But to be true to God and true to self, I cannot promise relief
Because I know I must write the truth, that is my belief

You can believe as you see fit, and choose your own path
I will not tell you that you are wrong or incite God's own wrath
Because I am told not to judge, and that everything good comes from God
That a house divided cannot stand, like a horse that is unshod

So when you judge you walk a line that is fine indeed
A line that is dangerous and will fill your life with need
Give your heart to each other in peace and in love
Let the Spirit descend to you from Heaven up above

Poetry by Brian Mullins

pea soup

I was writing that, I remember
As I page through the tabs of my browser
It was almost done, but not quite
Then I notice the notebook with half a poem
on the floor next to me
Grabbing a pen I quickly jot a line that pops
And get it out before it dissipates
Good Eats is on, Butter cream frosting
I love to make that stuff
That flashing light and beep
Ah a message from a good friend
Time to answer them
AFK a minute
One of the girls needs a tissue
Hey he's making pineapple cake now
I almost finished my dinner
Better warm it up
Hey.. when did I make these burritos
They are pretty stiff, must have been a few hours
Time to warm up my dinner
Ooh I didn't finish loading the dishwasher
Clink clutter bang
I'm coming with that Tissue!! Give me a minute
Better take my pills while I'm here
Get that tissue to the bedroom
Ooh look at the mess in the bathroom
All their towels and clothes in the floor
Better pick those up and hang them on the rack
So they don't mildew
Didn't I put a load of clothes in the washer last night?
Downstairs we go
Starting to smell, time to wash them again
Start it up

Authentic Perplexity

Upstairs again
Wait, I needed to finish the dishwasher
Ooh that's a good movie preview
Hey a message on my computer
I was writing that, I remember
As I page through the tabs of my browser
It was almost done, but not quite

Poetry by Brian Mullins

anguish

Sometimes I run and run through the night
Looking for the morning and the sunrise
But I don't find any release
As I dance along the pyramids of Egypt

Give into me and show me why
That these tunnels go from here to there
And how that you know the way
When you say you've never been here before

Tomorrow will bury all the blooms
A bulb of sorrow deep under the ground
And tonight we will search those rooms
Before the moon can make wide her sound
Because tomorrow will only deny
That tonight ever existed no
There will be no one who was high
And only upwards will we go

As we ride a float down the Nile
We can always plan on the Sun to shine
But as for this wanton trial
It will never make you yours or mine

Only when we accept each sign
As a Sanskrit blessing in the morning light
Only then can we heal the blind
Give the lost the wonder of their sight

When the sand begins to blow
And the camels falter in their step
Will we want for above or below
Only then will your eyes know their depth

Tomorrow will bury all the blooms
A bulb of sorrow deep under the ground
And tonight we will search those rooms

Authentic Perplexity

Before the moon can make wide her sound
Because tomorrow will only deny
That tonight ever existed no
There will be no one who was high
And only upwards will we go

With you by my side time will stop
Then only then will my world grow
As our eyes only raise on up
Only then will our souls really know

Tomorrow will bury all the blooms
A bulb of sorrow deep under the ground
And tonight we will search those rooms
Before the moon can make wide her sound

Because tomorrow will only deny
That tonight ever existed no
There will be no one who was high
And only upwards will we go

Poetry by Brian Mullins

unseen attackers

Stranded above the earth, this high tension tight rope
Shaking and vibrating with the force of unseen rape
Channeling the spirit of long dead actors and musicians
Looking for the Earth in every motion, every deed

As the morning sun rises, my pain is masked by fog
Sitting unobtrusive, hidden in a wall, potential for death
Oil reserves consumed in an effort to deny the fatality
Till probing hands seek it out for their own greed and lust

The world would survive without television, phones, AC
On solar winds we could ride through the universe unobscured
But comfort, a dragon of old, rears it's head and roars
And the world is destroyed yet again from inception

Authentic Perplexity

x-rays

You won't remember
Not in a few years
That you were even sick
Or that I held you
In that plastic tube
While they x-rayed your chest.
You won't remember
That torture device
Attached to a mini bicycle seat
That pressed against your sides.
You won't remember
That you cried
While staring in my eyes
As if to ask me why?
Daddy, why?
You won't remember
that moment when I broke
as my heart shattered
and my hands shook.
You won't remember
but I will never forget.

Poetry by Brian Mullins

downward spiral

It was daylight when last I checked, the skylight illumed by the Sun
But I sat here in my shell, while my inner self slowly began to consume
What was left of my happiness, and the twilight of day fades
And the bugs begin their melancholy song as they softly serenade

So I curl up into a ball and rise up my shield and stone walls
Not that I have any reason to be sad, I'm just going to fall
A moment ago thoughts of heat and steam pervaded all I was
Now just a dull ache of sadness creates my inner demise

Walk with me in the night as I slip into a pit of tar and ooze
Drowning my sorrow with a pill, some chocolate, some booze
Touch my hand as we journey into a land of darkness
From which there is no return to the light of day

Authentic Perplexity

abortion

Lost in the ocean of despair
An unborn child unwanted
Placed there by an unknown man
Hearts wrenched apart
Two horses teamed together
Abstinence such a cold thought
Denying ones own sexual pleasure
Shouldn't I be free from worry
And still obtain my own joy?
Life floats inside placed by two
On your back by choice this time
Yet the solution is the same
Justified by life's desire
Just an old dish in the fridge
Starting to grow
Thrown out
Father holds your hand
Pulls you into the room
Tells you to do it
Or get out
What choice have you
You're sixteen
No one understands
Everyone judges
Cry yourself to sleep tonight
As long as daddy can sleep
Mom will never know
How can we choose?
Either way we lose

Poetry by Brian Mullins

i saw heaven

As the dark settles above the glass
and the clouds move in front of the moon
I wonder to myself about life
Wars fought, lost, and began
forgotten, remembered, and stopped
All in the name of self predilection
Surrounded by florescent
A heater blaring in the kitchen
Baby snoring lightly with her giraffe
A moment, for just a moment
I see heaven
It's funny
I don't see Guns
I don't see tanks
I don't see weapons
I don't see killing
I don't see white
I don't see black
I don't see Asian
I see Love
Just for a moment
I saw heaven
I want to see it again

Authentic Perplexity

a prayer

Father, the Supreme Architect of the Universe,
And the Spirit, with her beauty and grace.
Our Lord Jesus, the Son, Saviour of mankind.
I ask you for your guidance
Your love and your support
Today and tomorrow, and always.
Give me the ability to forgive those
who I have not forgiven.
For I know there is a hardness in my heart.
I find it so hard to release
to let go these bitter feelings.
Though you have blessed me so greatly.
with love, family, children.
You keep me spiritually strong.
You keep me faithfully strong.
You open my eyes to the truth.
Help me to stay strong
Give to the needy
Comfort the pain ridden
And be the husband, father, and step dad
that you want me to be.

In honor of the Father,
In presence of the Holy Spirit,
And in the Name of Jesus Christ I pray.

Amen

Poetry by Brian Mullins

broken lawn mower

The lawn is rampant
A mini jungle filled with debris
All the roses are dieing from this plague
The one called winter in the mid-west
I see the plant matter piling up
Becoming moist and decayed
It reminds me of myself
Inside, rotting
As I clean dishes
Those miraculous cups
The ones that dirty themselves
Because no one used them
The door bell rings
A peal of the warden
To roll on two
I ease open the door
To see Fred
The neighborhood friend
The old man with no family
He smells of decay
I step outside
Easing the door shut behind me
The children fear him
He knows that but teases them
He's not dangerous
Just old
Alone
He has a wife
I see her drive him around
Sometimes
But most of the time
It's just him on his bench
Waving and yelling at the kids

Authentic Perplexity

Shaking his fist when they do something wrong
Yelling obscene stories to anyone who will stop
I wonder sometimes
If that will be me
Or if I'll be inside
Rotting
Like the roses
Until I am no more

Poetry by Brian Mullins

jigsaw woman

Though I may look
Like macramé lasagna
Broken and diffused
I am complete
Like a puzzle in a box
Jumbled and frazzled
But all 1000 mes are present
And accounted for
Don't try to work my puzzle
Just because it's on the table
If I wanted you to put me together
I'd ask you to
Just leave me in my box
Till I'm ready to share my pieces
To let you touch them
Because until then
If you touch my pieces
Your stealing them
Invading my private world
Raping my integrity
Hurting me
Nice guys don't put women back together
Nice guys don't finish last
Nice guys simply let women be themselves
Because nice guys know
That women aren't puzzles at all
They are boxes of beautiful pieces
And if we are lucky enough
And kind enough
And loving enough
And patient enough
She will open that box
And we will get to see all that makes her
Who she is

Authentic Perplexity

Poetry by Brian Mullins

the blacksmith

I remember.
How we used to hang out.
Me and the gang.
So many friends
That always were together.
I knew you forged knives.
It was an interesting trade.
Blacksmithing.
I always wanted to learn.
I never knew you'd put one in my back.
Sure we all had our fun.
All those parties
with the music
the drinks
the drugs.
All of us running from God.
Especially me.
It's a shame.
I cried once about it.
Wondering how you could betray me.
You were my friend.
She was my wife.
That doesn't matter for a seminary student
does it?
Did your study of God
Lead you to make me Uriah?
Were you to send me to the front lines?
So you could have what was mine?
Did you stare from your tower
into my garden?
All those years
spent in filth
up to our knees

Authentic Perplexity

except the one room
one room was always clean
can't make movies in a dirty room
so much laundry
so little time
so little detergent
I have moved on
but still it hurts
I really need a
washing machine
one for industrial loads
a front loader
one that can handle a lot of crap
At least now
while I air out my laundry
I'm not running anymore
I'm right here with God
with my real wife
my real soul mate
but you
where are you?
once my friend
where are you?

Poetry by Brian Mullins

i don't know

I don't know how I earned you, or why you're by my side
A beauty so exquisite, the thought of you makes me sigh
A pearl in the ocean, a starfish at high tide
The moon full in her beauty, does not your beauty vie

I seek to only be worthy of your love and grace
To be the man that you deserve, to light up your eyes with delight
Nothing moves my heart more than to see your lovely face
To hold you through the morning, and kiss you through the night

You are my completion, the other half of my soul
The yin to my yang, the apple to my eye
You are my soul mate, you make my heart whole
To love you fills my existence, lightens up the sky

Let me never think to take you for granted,
Nor to put you aside on a shelf to hide
Instead may our love be like a rose planted
In the middle of a path, not to the wayside

So to you my love I pledge, my dear wife
That every part of me is yours to use as you see fit
I promise you my heart, my life
May you never grow tired of it

Authentic Perplexity

silhouette

Your silhouette invades my mind
Like the morning sun creeping across the land
I seek for your touch like oxygen
Gasping for breath in a vacuum
Your lingering scent touches my soul
A constant reminder of the you that haunts me
I long to taste your glistening
For you make me whole
As we are One
Let us merge
Till tomorrow brings it's own light

Poetry by Brian Mullins

can you stand it?

It is so hard sometimes
not to attack
not to throw it back at you
so hard to stand and take
that relentless hail storm
that you send my way
bruised and battered
i crawl inside my shell
wishing to cut a jugular
to let the blood of hate
flow down my arms
to pummel you
a masochistic massage
what good would that do?
so i turn the other cheek
and hope I never run out of them

Authentic Perplexity

warning

Darkness, a foamy slime on top of a stagnant pool
Floating above my face as my body and soul separate
Pulling me down to my knees like an executioner
Brutal, bruising, haunting me, heartburn of the spirit

Foreign characters scribbled on the wall in blood
Simply forgotten, uncleaned, unnoticed
Placed by innocence, plagued by procrastination
Will life provide seduction for one so lame?

Nocturnal introductions of a carnal nature
Will they present themselves or fade into ether
Paranoia doesn't let the mind rest on Thursday
I am but a pawn, boxed in as you Castle

But remember my Wrath, as it boils in my conscious
I am your death, your destruction, your unbuilding
Atom by atom, separated by my gaze
Beware, for I am One, and you are unraveled

Poetry by Brian Mullins

did you cry?

Did you cry as you pierced his side?
As the water and blood flooded down your face
Were you concerned for your soul
As the soldier returned you to your place

Were you torn as his back you ripped?
Cleaving flesh from bone in a massive blow
Blood in rivulets flowing to the stone
As you watched in horror from down below

Did you shudder as you pierced his hand?
Your iron spine breaking bone and sinew
Did you feel his last brew shudder
As it was finished and his life discontinued

Did your ears ring as you shattered his knee?
Bone turned to dust bringing his weight on his chest
Breathing labored and difficult to continue
Or did you blame it on your wielder, was it his behest

Did you hear his words as in your arms he died?
Your oaken arms braced against the sun
As they pierced his hands and his feet
Attached to you was God's only Son

For you were the cross, the whip and spear
You pierced, flogged, and crucified
All because his truth you feared
Yet, not once you has he denied

So today I ask as the trigger was pulled
And life was taken with no reason provided
On your knees, in your car, at your desk, in bed
Did you cry as I cried?

Authentic Perplexity

unable to hurt

I tried this morning to be sad
To write a poem about despair
I wanted to express pain and hurt
As the wind blew through the trees
I could not sink my heart at all
Or even feel a twinge of guilt
As I watched the curving trunk
Of the sentinel in the yard
So I will resign myself
To happiness in my soul
And breath mindfully
Step with thought
Live with love

Poetry by Brian Mullins

Psalm 23

The Lord is my shepherd; I shall not want.
God fills me needs and my soul is complete
My prayers are answered, my need for life piquant
My filthy soul he cleanses, from worldly things I retreat

He maketh me to lie down in green pastures:
When anger fills my soul I need but walk in peace
Mindful of the blessings of Earth and nature
Giving in to the comfort that the Spirit does increase

He leadeth me beside the still waters
As the stream flows from its source to the ocean
My faith in the Architect never falters
For our life is but a flowing creek, to places unseen

He restoreth my soul
When I am need he lifts me up to bliss
Though life slowly takes it toll
Nothing can remove the Saviour's kiss

He leadeth me in the paths of righteousness for his name's sake
He shows me the path though the jungle threatens to devour
I will never misstep if I listen to his advice, and his footsteps I take
Just keep your footing sure, and wait for the final hour

Yea though I walk through the valley of the shadow of death,
And depression and despair seek to consume my Love,
I walk mindfully, conscious of every thought, every breath
And watch in every face, every tree, every plant for a sign from above

Authentic Perplexity

I will fear no evil: for thou art with me;
As the fruit is made of the sun, the wind, the rain,
Then we are made from everything else you see,
We are happiness, joy and pain
And inside the spark of divinity

They rod and they staff they comfort me
When I fear the world or the day to come,
I only have to look to my sentinel tree
Then his staff removes that which was cumbersome
and the Saviour with his yoke releases me

Thou preparest a table before me in the presence of mine enemies
I shall never hunger or have want for none
For the answer is but a prayer away, as I worship on my knees

Thou anointest my head with oil; my cup runneth over.
Sometimes I feel my cup has gone dry and bare
And I seek to hide my head under the cover
But the cup will not fill with sand and air
Nor with the touch of a lover
Only God can fill the hole that remains there
In your heart and your character

Surely goodness and mercy shall follow me all the days of my life:
Thou the world would have me believe I walk in vain
By ridiculing me and pushing me down, with trouble and strife
Trying to crush me with hardship and pain
A promise of eternal life
Is all that keeps me sane

And I will dwell in the house of the Lord for ever.

Amen

Poetry by Brian Mullins

Look for the Light

Many times I walk alone,
Waiting for morning light
Thinking my past to atone,
As I wander alone in the night.

Darkness makes me tremble,
and the chill of night I fear.
But I know it's just a preamble,
as I wipe away my tear

You see when everything goes wrong,
and your eyes begin to falter
You just have to be strong,
And your gaze cannot alter

Look forward to the morning,
family and friends are right.
Peace will come with no warning,
Just keep looking for the light.

Authentic Perplexity

a candle without a flame
by Brian Mullins & Dawn Rain

She called from the darkness, my beeswax Siren
A hopeless wail, causing my ears to bleed thought
Golden ringlets falling to her crystalline bed
Leaving my senses befuddled and distraught

Giving to my internal desires and needs
As I drown in a sea of helpless sound
Unforgiving, this succubus, this demon
As wisps of smoke rise swiftly from her crown

Just do it she calls, be the moth to my flame
Entangle yourself in my capacious nightfall
Bring hunger and appetite, whet your lust
Laughing at my ineptitude, life a tremble

My eyes absent, my hands betrayed
Away from this goddess I wrench
What is this demon without a flame
But a pricket impaling a wax wench

Poetry by Brian Mullins

poetry

Poetry is blood fluent upon my hands
writhing as maggots along my wrist
unable to dictate it's course of action
I am slave to it's predilection of pain
oozing from my pores
it's gangrenous beauty consumes me
exquisite lyrics produce waves
possessed by an ocean of elation
release is an eagle aflight
regal in it's splendor
endangered by our own foolishness
touch me intimately
for my mind is now a canvas sail
smooth and billowed by unseen wind
exciting this vessel in a northerly direction
towards the land of light
know my Spirit as I know yours
a dynamic epilogue to Self
My mind putrid with tallow
pain fog lathering words into gutters
yet I remain
a murderer
forced to spread blood
onto parchment

Authentic Perplexity

ogre

When I was in the field
they used to call me Shrek
because I was large
not just a little larger
I was ogreishly big
Not many ever compared to me
though occasionally
I met a fellow swamp beast
I guess that's why
I never felt worthy
never felt that I deserve her
but she told me
way back when
it wasn't for me to decide
who was I to make that choice
for her
she decided who was worthy
and she felt I was
I guess the one thing
that is good about an ogre
is having shoulders
broad shoulders
the better to support you with my dear
so remember my wife
I'll always be there
for you to lean on

Poetry by Brian Mullins

we are one

Your soul touches mine
like a flower touches the sun
stealing warmth for fuel
so natural it's unquestioned
pressed together
fields of snow
drifting across
the wind of your breath
lips parting in a painful gasp
an earthquake on my fault line
our minds brush together
for a moment we are One
your sensuous flood
moving like rapids
tossing me free of my craft
to flow wantonly with the current
bashing against the rocks
your body is the sun
burning me with each touch
my tongue blistered and sore
I crawl in submission
eyes like star light
twinkling afar
no longer focused
just drifting in the sea
can you feel me moving
like a rowboat at high tide
tossed to and fro
twisting and turning
struggling to stay afloat
until we are both tossed
into the flow
and begin to drown

Authentic Perplexity

in our ecstasy
to fade into darkness
in each others arms
no longer two
just us

Poetry by Brian Mullins

ignorance is death

So often we forget the world around us,
As the Sun and Moon twirl above our self absorbed ways,
When so much should astound us,
Yet we only worry about how much something pays

The forests, jungles, plains and seas,
Environments to corrupt while we fill our trays
The fish, the antelope, the lions, the trees
All we are concerned with is our movies, our plays

While life around us continues to die
And our heart is disconnected from our head
I have to wonder do we even try
To make a difference in the world before we are dead

But tonight under the full moon we are One
As the twilight passes through till dawn
For life must be born before it can come undone
To peace and love must our souls be drawn

Authentic Perplexity

unmatched

I see the weakness in your eyes
smell the fear in your heart
your trembling excites me
when you run
it just expedites my haste
wanton desert fills my nostrils
tearing at the ground
ripping like a tiller
a steel cable all that stands
between you and your death
your shouts obscene
as you dance and frolic
wanting you
needing you
your death
drool like rivers of sweat
unbidden, unwanted
I shall have you
my way will be complete
I am the alpha male

Poetry by Brian Mullins

i tasted you

i tasted you
last night
while you slept
as i floated above you
on the astral plane
you were gossamer
wings of a Luna moth
i could feel you
still on me after i left
your breasts were pearls
smooth and delicate
molded for centuries
your stomach an oasis
i but a traveler
lost in the desert
seeking that quenching liquid
i fall to drink
unable to compose
starvation knows no morals
a soothing rush
fills my mouth
taints my throat
makes me full
i am sated
by your lust
pausing to stare
at your sapphire eyes
my soul is yours
crimson fingers
encapsulate art
sculpture so divine
none can resist
i immerse myself

Authentic Perplexity

in your core
as your passion
surrounds my essence
i awaken
to find you were
there all along
beside me

Poetry by Brian Mullins

ancient knowledge

An ancient ceremony, seldom recorded
reminds of an art so beautiful and simple
healing the body mind and soul
it has one simple task
one simple move
but we over complicate it
daily we seek guidance
medicine and relief
we do ceremonies
rituals, dances, symbols
spells and more
poultices potions
pills and incense
when all we had to do
was get on our knees
and realize
we are healed

Authentic Perplexity

fantasy, reality, dreams

Did you taste me on your lips
as you passed the door to death
letting your mind wander the ether
into the oblivion of night
I wandered the pattern in Amber
as you passed the night in slumber
Dworkin laughing in the chilled air
a stag, a man, a dwarf
a madman's ravings gone awry
We walked the path of heroes
as we traveled with a wizard and a vampire
to a land far away
a battle for all mankind
fought on a ground of pure evil
I also slept at your side
in a desert, under a tarp
while the flies surrounded
in the sweltering heat
chewing us like bubble gum
but eventually
we will wake
to Band aids
dog manure
and pizza crust

Poetry by Brian Mullins

burning

*I feel a burning in the pit of my stomach
an echo of thing past and future
looking for an escape from a petrified domain
as my body spasms in submission
holiday spent and forgotten
disappointment and disdain
puppies that are monsters
children that are full grown
food that never stays in place
consciousness is fleeting
but rest, it never comes*

Authentic Perplexity

ultimate sacrifice

On the cross he hung
Our sins for all to atone
Covenant fulfilled

Poetry by Brian Mullins

dream

Last night was a cold, lazy spring night.
As the evening chill began to set in
a procession passed, moving with the wind.
Their head lights were on to light the way
Though there was plenty of light left from day.
I wasn't sure where it was going
Or where it had been. There was no way of knowing
who was in that car, laid out in a box
made of pine and wood. Was it a hoax
that this motorcade chose to pass along
so close to twilight. Was I wrong
to think of the nightfall of life?
How we pass through life with such strife?
This morbid chariot pulled to a close
and the stench of decay assaulted my nose.
Was this some kind of prank
a morbid April fools with a scent so rank?
I approached the car and peered inside
where this funerary box of tree chose to reside.
Through the viewing pane i began to see
that this funeral procession was for me

Authentic Perplexity

where am i?

here i am i called from my corner of pious chastity
knowing i would receive no answer in return
one would think that i was guilty of blasphemy
the silence so brutal, i'm starting to burn

my heart a hermit crab crawling for the sea
as vacationing children run searching for treasure
one passing by simply stepping on me
my crushed agony his childhood pleasure

yesterday we were on the moon for a while
jumping kangaroos skipping with glee
why this sudden impetuous trial
today on Jupiter, crushed by the gravity

this new puppy dancing with delight
to perform my masters every whim
till the joyful day turns towards night
and my masters eyes grow dim

behind the house on a chain i reside
as snow begins to fall on my moist nose
but i dare not disturb those inside
for fear of the belt or the hose

this pain i feel on this lonesome eve
might have an easement in store
for i feel now i'm a pet peeve
i used to be collectible, no more

an opened package of a childhood toy
that one day would be worth much
opened for the pleasure of a boy
ah the tactile sense of touch

but if his pleasure was genuine
then worth millions it would be
for his worth is greater than mine
just wish someone still wanted me

Poetry by Brian Mullins

malibu barbie

I watched with horror in my eyes
As they formed to societies lies
Nothing given nothing gained
But the notion left me pained

Six wonderfully formed women
But none the one she wanted then
All laying at the bottom of the box
Because they didn't form the fox

Too pale, too blond, too red
Painted on bruises, with ink and lead
But she needed the sandy blond tan
As only Malibu Barbie can

Ah they learn so young to see
With the eyes of society
Innocence gone and prejudice forms
As we all conform to societies norms

Authentic Perplexity

crystal in the sky

I don't know what will come next
From this gaping orifice
I just know the will behind it
Is not on the surface

I trust in him so much
I give him my core
How can that be enough
I just want to give more

On my knees I have been
Since my song I had heard
The Source of compassion
Mediation on the word

Longing for release
Of this pain held inside
Like an ostrich in the sand
I only want to hide

I see it in a crystal shroud
As the moon passes above
A shimmering soul trapped
Fearing God's Love

I am here for you my friend
A crutch for the lame
I have been there my friend
I have felt the same

Poetry by Brian Mullins

your buttons

You know I like it when I push your buttons
Touching those spots that make you humid
How your neck smells when your pulse races
Lavender and honey, eyes and need lucid

Your knees like Jello, dropping to the floor
Weakness, a poison creeping through
Body alive, a seizure of passion
Thighs damped by the taste of your dew

Ballet of fingers across your pleasure trail
While my tongue writes a symphony
One note at a time proceeds
This Dode knows no sympathy

Only one thing that I ask at this time
Grant me one thing with your breath
Shower me with your tipple
Let me taste your little death

Authentic Perplexity

laments

The moment I held you for the first time
I knew that you were mine.
That till the end of time I would be
There as long and as much as I could.
Here tonight I watched as you
Spiked up and down
Scared out of my mind
While others told me what to do
Because I didn't know
Because I didn't know
That's when I realized
If you died...
I think I would too

Poetry by Brian Mullins

silence

i fear it
all of my being
the dreams
they come at night
dark loathsome things
eating at my insides
raking at the wall
like rats in a cage
there must be evil inside
misery doesn't come to good
lightning, chasing darkness
thunder, chasing silence
reprieve from myself
until tomorrow

Authentic Perplexity

in the night

A dark raven descends upon me
Fangs bared for my soul
Repentant knees calloused with use
A razors edge on my eye
Give me toxic waste to drink
For I cannot bear purity
Water no longer quenches
World wide my happiness dies
How can One live and not know pain
My heart is diamond
So hard it breaks easily
Fractured and flawed
By children dieing
Give me hope
Show me why man decides
to put his pleasure before their life
Show me why?

Poetry by Brian Mullins

gravity

I feel the weight of sin on my shoulders
Not just my own but yours as well
Know experience has shown me
What some call a personal hell
Once a man experienced
All our sin and our pain
Do you ever feel the same?
Like those children dieing
every 3 seconds from aids and famine
Like you were holding a bowl of
oatmeal just out of the reach the entire time
How can one not be aware of the
suffering of the world and be alive
I am that dark cloud
The one floating in front of the storm
Leading the way for the funnel
That strips you from your home
I am that spark
From the frayed cord on your iron
The one that burns down your house
And takes all your clothes
I am that drunk driver
That hit your cousins little girl
I am that bastard who mistreated you
who beat you in your bed
Whipped you till you bled
I am that man who stole your money
Leaving you without the ability
To pay for your child's education
I am that earthquake
That took your home
Destroyed your family
Your friends

Authentic Perplexity

I am that mountain lion
That attacked your cousin
Leaving nothing but a shoe
I am that doctor
Who performed that abortion
I am the one who cut into your head
I am the one who killed you, dead
How can I repent, for all these sins
God will forgive me
That is promised
But can I forgive myself

I am sorry for all of it

I am sorry

Poetry by Brian Mullins

know thyself

I know that inside me lies the Kingdom of God
Some will never realize this and think me quite odd
For how can one be so in tune with the Spirit
One only has to be still, and then they will hear it

That voice inside that calls to the Soul of man
That wisdom is inside you and access it you can
You just must release all your preconceived mind
Release your notions, and freedom is the Divine

See with your eyes, and feel with your hands
Do not tempt God or make false demands
Simply realize that you're part of the One
The Father, The Spirit, The Son

For life is too short to debate away
Questioning God can go on all day
But knowing the Truth without a doubt
Is enough to make anyone stand up and shout

You have inside you the power to heal
Liberty inside and God granted free will
So look to your Soul and your inner light
And God will teach you what is wrong and right

Authentic Perplexity

rubber-necking

an echelon of ducks
bobbing their beaks in unison
apriorism of the masses
obtuse to dolor of neighbors
ah that empathy were not barren
that more persist in residence
acquiescent to civil producers
instead, gory adulation of displacement
bread crumbs become deification

Poetry by Brian Mullins

rose among thorns

It is a hard thing for man to dream
About what an angel might think
Upon viewing a girl still in her prime
Baggage some call it
Those extra nuances that make her
who she is today
You see she's been through so much
She has experienced a mans touch
Her beauty though still stands out
From under the layers of makeup
Applied with a paint knife
Plaster over wire mesh
Walking down deserted streets
Men looking her up and down
Wondering if she is loose
Just because she is alone
That is the card she has been dealt
The death trump
Who would think she was considering
ending it all
Razors in the cabinet
A Valium that doesn't end
Her hair curled with a nine dollar
curling iron from Wal-Mart
Collar turned high against the wind
What would an angel think
Of this Rose among the thorns

Authentic Perplexity

a thought

A thought in my mind, both bothersome and kind
Does my heart know the answer or only divine
I seek and search, for the promise was made
Knock and it shall be opened, the promise he gave

Philosophies abound, and religions innumerable
Dogmas so vast, and enlightenment so variable
Taught by rote, or taught by inspiration
Some dance, some sing, some worship with perspiration

But all those questions, that have been posed before
Are all just enigmas that tend to close the door
All the time, we ask do we believe in Him
Some answer verbose, some answer trim

Today I ask a question, that as of yet was unheard
About the shepherd who wants to collect his herd
Ask all we want do you believe in God, that you can
But I want to know, does God believe in man?

Poetry by Brian Mullins

paradox

Why did God create man, only to fall
Knowing the thoughts, the answers to all
Putting the apple in the garden to consume
Knowing the outcome, God does not assume

Was Adam to blame when he ate this fruit
After Eve offered did he not intuit
From the garden expelled into this world to toil
To work and sweat, gather and till soil

Or was it the blame for Eve who seduced
Asked him to eat the pome she produced
After all she picked it, knowing in the end
The result would be expulsion, living in sin

Or was it the fault of Satan who tempted the mind
Knowing the weakness of all humankind
Man's lust for woman over powering his heart
That once aroused we aren't that smart

Each person can place the blame on who they will
But first you must consider the entire deal
God is omnipresent, through time and space
He doesn't exist in just one place

Transcending all time, existing as One
Knowing the result before it was done
Because of this fact, you realize his love of man
Was known before creation, as only God can

Authentic Perplexity

You see he loved you before he made you,
As a child to a mother, that she already knew
Could you give her up, with the love you have now
If you experienced that love before her conception some how

Loving you before creation, because he was after it too
Existing in all times, lets give credit where it is due
God made us not to fail and not to fall
It made us because he loved us, that was all

Loving he made us all with free will
So the decision we made, were made to seal
The fate of man of his own mind and choice
So do not lament, do not strain your voice

Eve was to blame because she offered the fruit
Adam was to blame because he soon followed suit
Satan was to blame, he tempted us of his own volition
So we are all to blame for our prohibition

The next time you wonder why God made us so
Remember he knew you from head to toe
Before he ever thought of making our kind
He already knew us inside his omniscient mind

Poetry by Brian Mullins

innocence lost

I see her eyes alive with delight
As she senses digits aligned with sight
A double rainbow above her head
Colorful patchwork makes up her bed

Her fingers touch each textured fabric
With the diligence of a childhood rubric
Giraffes, tigers, bears, and more
Floating above her as she graces the floor

Kicking her feet and laughing with joy
As she realized it was she who moved the toy
Cause and effect we take for granted
But her vision isn't yet so slanted

To see with the eyes of a child
Once again to feel the earth so wild
As flowers bloom and blades of grass grow
Or hands make puppets on a childhood show

Can you imagine all the wonder and awe
Things once seen, that we never really saw
So I look around and try to imagine how it feels
To experience again her first flavored meals

To taste God's grace from the lowest of stature
Before we forget harmony and then we mature
Puberty both a blessing and a curse to man
So enjoy it my child while you still can

And to the rest of the world this I charge
Try not to look at things like you are so large
Get down low, and experience for the first time again
The world from purity the world without sin

Authentic Perplexity

early morning intrusion

*I wasn't sure how to feel
trapped in my own nakedness
pressed against passion
innocence a few inches from heat
pushing sincerity away
was a dagger to my heart
moods destructed in the night
awake, languid, in a stupor
typing thoughts of yesterday
polyphagia of virtue
maternal screams at 2 am
no respect for person
canine betrayal of sanctity
the throne room defiled
as I sit clothed
still naked in the night*

Poetry by Brian Mullins

not so simple

seems so easy, those simple words
cast your burdens on me, my yoke is light
try as i might the burden sticks right here
maybe it is fuel for me, maybe i am meant to write

this pain inside, arthritic wounds
maybe not ever meant to heal
Job in his strength was more man than i
often wonder how that would feel

to be so strong that despite my wounds
still worshiping with soul and might
children dead, fortunes gone, wife obtuse
all taken like a thief in the night

here i complain about pain in my legs
a stomach ache i cannot control
when all that is in me, cries out to him
help save this pour wretched soul

some say because my faith isn't strong
my afflictions have come from my sin
they couldn't be further from the truth
my afflictions come from within

i believe with my soul and mind
with my heart and all that i am
in God, Jesus, the Holy Spirit
and the universal master plan

so here i set, desolate
in a painful daze
this swelling, red, pain infest
has gone on for days

Authentic Perplexity

tomorrow i pray, let me be
for much more i cannot take
release me from these demons Lord
please Lord, for my spirits sake

Poetry by Brian Mullins

spirit walker

i'm not sure who i am to be honest
at this moment in time i am a ghost
living behind the lines of morality
feeding off the spiritual energy of my host

my essence is that of a Mandaen scribe
lost forever in his own field of dreams
searching every moment in time for Spirit
echoed in his laughter, his tears, his screams

am i worthy of this thing called Spirit
can i even hear it's call?
are any of us worthy of this Spirit
anyone worthy at all?

i call out in my sleep for knowledge
for God to show me the way
but in the end i end up falling
into that same bitter malaise

a journey of epic proportions
from this shore to that far one
why not bend reality a bit
take one step and i'm done

but that age old fear of worthlessness
presses me against the wall
raping me of my consciousness
making me feel three inches tall

was she right in what she said
those past years in my mind
not worthy of love or acceptance
not ever, not my kind

i seek to right wrongs
that i never once commit
maybe one day on this journey
worthiness will transit

Authentic Perplexity

don't fear for me my friend
for my salvation is guaranteed
don't fear for yourself either
just those words you must heed

it's not the destination that concerns me
nor doubt in my mind of his light
it's the journey from here to yonder
through the darkness of night

you see i am a poet
who cannot see the dark
though it is in front of him
naked, brutal, stark

it tends to sneak it's way inside
and rot me from my core
never satisfied with misery
darkness wants more

virgin to my ancestry
my totem only guessed
unable to trace lineage
a mutt describes me best

no ghost dance, no drum song
no great spirit chant in the night
great temples built in earthen shantis
screams till the morning light

i am no spirit walker
nor am i near my end
for another journey awaits me
each time i use this pen

Poetry by Brian Mullins

drawing a blank

At the dawn of our lives, we are as a canvas
Smooth, unwritten, unformed, unmolded
Then experience, pain, love and hardship
Being cherished, nourished and scolded

We become who we are one step at a time
Till the adult that we were destined to be is made
Living on sayings, and things we were taught
If life gives you lemons make lemonade.

Individuals with notions that are their own
but formed of those of their parents and friends
Our minds are but replicas of former art works
our thoughts a means to ends

When will we see the next Picasso
Einstein who cannot tie his shoes?
The master musician with his grand piano
Or the singer of rhythm and blues

The writer of hymns and gospels
A dancer who makes the world spin
A teacher, a prophet, a Master
Will there be another without sin?

So here tonight a masterpiece I want to write
But my mind is drawing a blank, a stall
So I sit here, right where I started
A blank canvas, no paint, nothing at all

Authentic Perplexity

asparagus

My succubus bids me approach, with her lewd dance of coitus,
Though I have been there before, I did not garner enlightenment.
Grabbing and pulling, licking my fingers like a child
Candy cotton spun into a pornographic film for my seducing
The heat of passion filling my senses no room for sanity
My vain attempt at control nothing more than a gnat on an elephant
From the start I knew the malaise that taste would bring
Yet taste of this fountain of gall until I was thoroughly profligate
My senses battered by my own admission yet unable to comply
No analgesic, no anesthetic, nor even a tranquilizer at my aid
So suffer I must at my own demise, no stay of execution
Ah that I might have lived privation instead of gluttony exposed
Instead in this puddle of my sin, I shall remain until morrow

Poetry by Brian Mullins

ponder this

How can one speak of God?
It's like trying to tell a child
what ginger ale tastes like.
It's bitter. It's sweet. It fizzes.
It tastes like root beer but not.
It tastes like ginger, but not.
They will never know what it
tastes like from that description.
Would you? Would you think fondly
of ginger ale from that description?
Would it make you reminisce of that flavor?
Jesus can speak of God.
Jesus has experienced God.
He's seen him.
The Holy Spirit she can talk of God.
She has known God for her existence.
So the only way we can
speak of God, is through
second hand experience?
From the Holy Spirit,
we can be guided towards God.
And we can speak with authority
of the Holy Spirit.
Living as Jesus did we can
experience the Christ in us,
and then we can speak of authority
about Jesus, the Christ.
But what does speaking
about Christ do? Arguing about him?
Telling how we feel inside?
Nay it does no good to
quote scripture at someone
who has never felt the Spirit.

Authentic Perplexity

*They must experience it
themselves.
Jesus is a bulb
in the heart of a man.
We can cultivate it,
show it how to live,
show it Christs' words that
it might blossom forth.
But we cannot make it grow.
We cannot tell you how it feels.*

You must experience it.

*I can tell you what Agape is
to me
to myself
to I
but will you know Agape
until you have experienced it?*

*I can tell you what Dode is
the arousal
the perfume of her scent
the orgasmic completion
the ecstasy of holding her after
the ecstasy of holding her during
but will you know Dode?*

*I can tell you many things
how it felt that first time I rode my motorcycle.
Free as the wind.
Dancing with death
No helmet, just me and the power
1000cc of engine between my legs.
metallic virility
But you won't know till you
feel it for yourself.*

So I challenge you

Poetry by Brian Mullins

Search for it
Seek it
See it

Do not say it does not exist.
For if you have no proof it doesn't,
and you have no proof it does,
and you have not experienced everything,
then you cannot deny that there is a chance
that it is there.

Experience it.

Just something else to ponder

Authentic Perplexity

sounds of silence

I remember walking through the land of ether
Listening to the cold crisp air as it crackle against my soul
I wasn't sure who I was looking for, but I knew I'd find her
But the chill was quickly masticating my muscles, taking it's toll

A golden boulder the size of a small town came by
I was sure that it would hit me, but then it came to stop
A will-o-wisp popped out and spied my eye
The hill you are looking for, she is at the top

The darkness was a barrier, a wall of sheer veneers
But atop the mound I saw my golden, sparkling treasure
She rest upon a pedestal, made of crystal and tears
Her hair was made of heartaches and pleasures

I asked her for a name, and she laughed a song
A twinkle of faith, music so pure it made me die
To have a name to such beauty as this would be wrong
Because you see, what I was looking at was you and I

Poetry by Brian Mullins

~~misery~~

*Depression
my mistress
insatiable*

*dance
upon my corpse
at dawn*

*for tonight
we are
a pigeon roost*

*tomorrow
is our
bedding*

Authentic Perplexity

new sheets

Did your mind swirl as you gaped into the abyss?
Were you blown away with the tendrils of lust?
Was your mind a fantasy dismissed?
Of the sweat, the aroma, the dust

Give into me with your hearts desire,
As your passion fills my soul
Break into me, as we perspire
While Dode takes it's toll

We are the phoenix from the ash
Consumed by our own heated lechery
Mind full of filth, mind full of trash
Oh how can a heart handle such treachery

Writhing in sheets of soft jersey beech
My tongue does dance through your anatomy
Your inner workings my taste buds seek
From the organ of your skin, to the edge of cytology

Taste me as I taste you,
Till the light of morning comes.
When the drops of wettest dew
Our hearts will beat as one

Poetry by Brian Mullins

just words

Remember that song we sang as children?
The abc song? How we danced and laughed.
Little did we know that we were learning runes of power.
With just a few combinations
we could tear someone from limb to limb.
Four letters is all it takes
cunt
slut
dick
sometimes three
ass
five can crush
bitch
whore
some can kill
fagot
then there are those who go for vein or artery
they aren't happy with just words
sentences of death and doom
Go to hell you fagot
Suck my dick bitch
Go take your cunt and sell it you whore
but we had a few other words
that I remember growing up
four letter words
love
five letter words
buddy
six letter words
forget
seven letter words
forgive
but there was a three letter word

Authentic Perplexity

that we used to say
and I always thought it went in the second list
of good words and good things
but apparently it has been moved to top
with the sluts, bitches, and whores
the three letter word was

God

Poetry by Brian Mullins

springtime joy

My nest of newspaper built to last
Filled with broken eggs of last years hatch
Stolen from another nest and placed into ours
Watched and cultivated, waiting for hours

Spring time came and with it the dew
The morning sun, through our leaf canopy shines through
Their wings are untested but away they fly
Not noticing me left behind a tear in my eye

A robin am I, with a red stain on my chest
My own blood dripping down, but it's for the best
As in their red chariot they escape for the day
On the way to the nest they prefer, one made of straw or hay

I preen and I prune, while away they soar
Till the nest is pure and ready for more
An eternity later they return for a time
A time that I thought was ecstasy sublime

The nest is ruined and destroyed once again
By their own feet, and admission, they feel it's no sin
This nest they wish to leave and never return
Because it's a mess, when will they learn?

When one shits in his own bed,
Then that is where he chooses to lay his own head.
He can't escape from that mess he has made,
Isn't that an ace calling a club a spade?

Authentic Perplexity

bittersweet sharp

there is a hole in my heart
where your words passed through
your tongue bittersweet sharp
no defense, nothing i could do

you shot me in the back
when you said what you said
so matter of fact
made me wish i was dead

this place makes you unhappy
because of the state that it's in
you could have slapped me
or hit me, even then

how can i make you love this
when i can't even compete
with the perfection that his is
i am sorrow complete

shadows of jelly beans fog minds
and technological gadgets
movies of all kinds
if you want it he'll have it

i can only offer you my love
and treat you with kindness
but like a homing dove
i will always be less

i don't want to be a facsimile
nor do i want to be a dream
just to make you smile
i just want to scream

Poetry by Brian Mullins

my burden is light

When your down in the dark damp place,
And the tears cover your moistened face.
As your alone in the dark and sad,
Remember the times we've had

There was a time when I was all alone,
When my sins I thought I could not atone.
Then I realized that you were I and I was me
When you hurt, I hurt too you see

Come to me and let me share your pain
Let me see your face in the rain
Hold each other as friends do aright
Till the warmth has passed us through the night

He said his yoke was easy and his burden light
That we can take his yoke if we hold on tight.
We are the body of Christ you see.
It's my job to help lift you up, with me

Take my yoke and let me have yours for a while
Till you realize that we carry the same in style
For our burdens are the same, you see
For I am you, and you are me

Namaste

Authentic Perplexity

silent turbidity

I always hated silence
The absence of sound
Made me feel I was absent from reality.

I surrounded myself with noise
A fan at night so I could sleep
A TV when no one was around
The radio blaring, the tune didn't matter

I felt so alone
When silence surrounded me
Crushing me with it's weight.

Today it is silent.
I don't need a Television murmuring in the background.
I don't need a radio playing unknown music.
I don't even need a fan to keep me company.

I realized last night during meditation
That I am part of the whole.
I am part of the One.
I am never alone.
Silence is a reminder.

A reminder to listen.

Poetry by Brian Mullins

repentant sojourner

I confess to you my friends, for you are as much a priest as I
I confess to you my sins, apparently they need to be before I die.
I won't die tomorrow or Thursday, and probably not today
Before I do though, there are a few things I'd like to say

I'm sorry I killed the grasshopper, with my b.b. gun when I was three
I buried it myself you know, there I knelt on my knee
I'm sorry it didn't get to live to have a family of it's own
All because I wanted to shoot something, to kill was the zone

I'm sorry that I hit my brother, with a stick when I was ten.
We think I broke his hand, but we didn't tell even then.
I swung in anger and with rage, that was out of line
If any hand should have been broken it should have been mine.

I'm sorry that I didn't take my poodle to the vet myself.
I just put it in my mental files, and stored it on the shelf.
I'm sorry that he died in her arms, and that I will never know.
If he could have been saved, if more tenderness did I show?

I'm sorry that I didn't want to go places after work,
I just wanted to sit down and eat my dinner, grab my knife and fork
I know you'd been there all day long, and wanted to get out
But all I did was play my games, maybe even shout

I'm sorry that I don't stay happy every hour of the day
I'm sorry that when my brain works, it works in it's own way
That when I wake in the morning, your not always the first on my mind
That when you need a shoulder, I'm not always so kind.

That when I walked through the forest of the state parks of VA
I didn't look around me, I just trudged on in my way
There were so many beauties that I might have just seen
If only more aware of myself, and the world I had been

Authentic Perplexity

I'm sorry that I irritated so many of you in jest,
Maybe your anger and our separation was for the best.
The quaint things I did to try and make amends,
Weren't just fashionable, they weren't just trends

They were from the heart and from the soul of a man on a path
As the jungle of life, with the machete of hope, I cut my swathe
But rejected they were and rejected they shall be
Until the end of time, when at judgment we shall see

That I am but a humble man, with a humble lesson to teach
I do not pretend to be a scholar, nor do I proffer to preach
I am just here to love, and to be friend
Until my life has been offered up, and to the Spirit I send.

Poetry by Brian Mullins

chewing gum

I saw her standing there, across the street.
She had her hair cut short, around her chin.
A light auburn color complimented by blond highlights.
Her sleek figure outlined in work clothes.

She tilted her head to the side the way she always does,
Looking down at the kids. Smiling. Playing.
I longed for her. More than that, I longed for That.
All of it. No matter the consequences, the hardships.

I avoided like an old man avoids a child with a cold.
Only doing what I was asked, doing what I was told.
The bastard might see, me stalking out here.
Might think it odd, might think it queer.

What right does he have to control her life?
He's just a fool, she's no longer his wife.
Control is the issue, will she gain it back?
Will it help if I tell her I'll pack?

I sleep in the parking lot of a Wal-Mart
As the busy unknowns push their shopping carts
Waiting for a time when he's unaware.
A time when he won't stop and stare.

I am wanted, yet trash. No one has claimed
An old puppy, ran over and maimed.
When will I find a home, a heart to accept
All of my failures, my heart aches, my depth

A flower she is, growing in a tangled web
As the tide flows, she blooms and she ebbs
One moment she's mine, free and alive
Next she is gone, and she's afraid to dive

Today I am gum, on the bottom of the desk
Put here after being chewed, results of a test.
Accepted for all my flaws, and part of her core
How can I help her, to see that she's more

Authentic Perplexity

She's not a bruised apple, waiting for decay
She's the light of the morning, the light of my day
Just one thing is all that I ask of you my love.
Don't put me under the desk, let me hide above

Poetry by Brian Mullins

worms on a sidewalk

As I sit in this hollow expanse
surrounded by turgid thoughts
my mind is filled with peace
a tranquility so divine
that it can only be from above.
I hear the soft murmur of my children
playing in the yard. The baby in her bouncer
the dog, snoozing the noon day sun.
The squeal of giant automatons
pierces the halcyon atmosphere
breaking the reverie of my soul.
A bird builds it's nest in a tree
by our front stoop each year.
I wonder if it notices the metallic clash
the thunder of the passing train
the rumble of thunder in the distance
Or is it content with being.
Content with being with One.
Knowing it's purpose is to
feed it's young and bring forth new life.
Content with that existence.
She doesn't need television.
Or a blog. Or a journal. Or a blue pill.
She's just happy building that nest,
repairing it after winter. Filling it with eggs.
After a rainstorm the worms, they crawl
all over our sidewalk. Like us in our everyday lives.
Walking through the chilled night air
I try to step over them least I crush one out of existence.
Just like our everyday lives.
We crawl along in a hurry to escape
the saturated soil of our house, our jobs,
our stress. Meanwhile the giants of

Authentic Perplexity

*bureaucracy stamp above us. How many
of these take time not to stamp out our existence.
How many of you are worms....
How many of you will be gone tomorrow...
Stamped out by life...
be ever watchful, every wonderful, ever filled
with awe and reverence. Life is filled
with beauty and lessons.*

*We like a young babe may learn.
We must teach ourselves to do the
most basic of things.*

We must learn to see.

Poetry by Brian Mullins

your blushing

I can feel you writhing, under my gaze
Knowing what I want but neither of us able to take
Your mind a fog, my mind a daze
You must think me a brigand, a thief, a rake

I steal your innocence with my eyes
While my soul rapes your core
My inner being spreading your thighs
While your eyes plead no more

I can smell your scent, lavender and honey suckle
Your heavenly aroma fills the room
I can't help but chuckle as I chase you
Towards your impending doom

The corner I catch you, out of breath and unarmed
Too weak to defend yourself from my attack
You realize too late that your already charmed
As you spread your fingers across my back

A tantalizing kiss, a war of the tongues
As we ravish each other with our eyes and mouth
A shuddering breath escapes your lungs
As my hand probes further south

I break away at the last minute, knowing my work is complete
It's time for you to leave for work and time for me to sweep
For I know that now your soul is lust replete
I have only to wait and to sleep

Authentic Perplexity

~~masticating~~

Marble white, the stones of demise
Breaking, gnashing, destroying all in their way
Their purpose to break and grind
As they pulverize all that pass through

But the beauty is often missed
Of this destructive deluge.
Nourishment provided for all
Giving peace and refuge

Masticate with your heartbeat
While your breath is smooth and counted
Let not any moment of any persons life
Be for naught or discounted

As the muscles work together to perform a feat
So the boulders pulse and an avalanche ensues
For your mind is in need of nourishment
And nourishment is what issues

Poetry by Brian Mullins

butterfly

Sometimes we look to a pill,
To answer our earthly woes.
Other times we look to a bottle,
To help numb us to our toes.

Then we look to our friends,
To talk and get our feelings out.
Sometimes we write it down,
Next we scream and shout.

The butterfly lays her egg,
A cocoon of silk and strands.
Inside it comforts and soothes,
Until it's constraints are more demands

You see the answer is not without,
The answer has never been.
Though it helps to write, scream and shout
Talk to a friend, search, even then.

A bulb under ground, takes root
A small green sprout begins to grow
It takes help from without
And remains comforted by the dirt in the snow.

Then in spring, when safety has arrived
A green sprout again shoots forth
It displays it's dress and garments
Again filled with wonder and worth

You see we are that flower, that worm in a cocoon
We are wrapped in comfort provided by love, friends, even sleep
But depression is our hinderer, our winter filled with snow
So reach inside for that divine spark, that part that is you nestled so very deep

Authentic Perplexity

Emerge from the darkness covered in glory and splendor
Show the world your colors and new found bloom
Spread your wings and fly my butterfly
For your beauty will always out shadow the gloom

Poetry by Brian Mullins

sometimes

Sometimes I think life isn't worth living, and that I can't go anymore
That death has shut me in the closet and has barricaded the door
That life is just an empty pit, a grave filled with dismay
I couldn't bare it if I had to go on, to live another day

Then I notice the life around, the intricacies of the Earth
The fragility of the flower, the great tree and it's girth
How that everything has been made with a precision not of man
Everything was made unto a master plan

The ratio of phi, and the complexity of the eye
The way that our mind works, that there is a You and I
The beauty of a new born child, learning each and every thing new
The beauty of each person, strangers, lovers, You

The sun as it rises and paints the forlorn sky
So many colors, so pleasing to my eye
Dickenson said it was a broom that splayed this fancy paint
Colors that artists replicate, but whose beauty cannot taint

A flower in the garden, with dew from the morning drop
As they gently flow down the stalk and on the ground they stop
To replenish the earth and bring forth life anew
All this in our garden of Earth, made for me and You

So when these thoughts I cannot fight, and despair I do find
I look towards the mirror, and see with my heart and mind
Could I have made something so intricate, beautiful and complex
As this thing we call the face, our inner workings, our matrix

We all have our moments, when life is filled with gloom
When all our mind can think of is, hate, death, and doom
But look towards the earth to show you that life is filled with Love
That somewhere, someplace, somehow, there is someone up above

Authentic Perplexity

bed bugs

it's Monday, eight in the morning.
spring break started
the kids are home for a week
thought i might sleep in this morning
then the bed bugs started to bite
horrible little monsters these
making terrible noises
scratching at your back
yelling and clawing and kicking
how can one ignore that?
i tried, i tried to ignore it and go back to sleep
then the kids came in
and stated playing with the bed bug
getting it all excited
time to get up, no more sleep for me
and who can get mad at a bed bug?

Poetry by Brian Mullins

tears of this clown

It's funny how words can be a hammering blow
That one single phrase can hurt more than a bomb
The thought crosses my mind do you even know?
That your words have sealed me in my tomb

I tried to dedicate something to your soul,
A testament of how I feel deep inside.
As I stare into that deep dark bowl,
To try to discern my future and decide.

I am but a weary traveler, who has stopped to bring you love
And the road is long and rugged, to much so to travel alone.
I thank the Lord and the Angels above,
To be a part of this our life, this our home.

Just sometimes I wonder if you feel the same,
As a dagger pierces my side.
An off comment here or there, without a name,
The pain is often too much to hide.

I read too much into what you say,
I hear things that may not be there.
But every morning, every day
I show my love in this snare

Peace to you my love, as you live with me
That your heart will be filled with wonder and awe
Just I hope that one day you will see
The words that I have written, and the vision I saw

Authentic Perplexity

i am

As a leaf in the fall, hanging by a thread
Fluttering in the breeze, all life appearing dead
The wind blows me round, moving me as it will
I am

A bulb underground, life to renew
A passion in heart, trying to subdue
A fragrant herb, thyme, oregano, dill
I am

A stream of confetti at a maritime parade
A competitive soul trying to charade
A hard working man in a saw mill
I am

A poem on a page, writing in the dark
A drawing in a book, contrasting and stark
An artist writing down his thought with a quill
I am

Darkness falling quickly on a mid summers eve
A vacation quickly over, no one wanting to leave
Hope in the future of the polar bear, the seal
I am

An inventor alone a light bulb over his skull
A baby falling asleep to her mothers sweet lull
The colors of the spectrum from white to teal
I am

A rock in the forest, covered with years of moss
A mother in a rocker, grieving for her loss
A contractor trying to strike a million dollar deal
I am

Part of the cosmos the universe as an ark
Every single atom, every quark, every spark
A thought in the mind of a prophet unfulfilled
We are.

Poetry by Brian Mullins

what would i say

Join me today as we usher in an era of peace,
For a world where violence and war will cease.
Join hands today for and end of a phase,
For now we shall have peace till the end of our days.

An epiphany of dreams brought forth in an instant,
Where love and harmony are our constant.
A world in which fantasy is no longer a desire,
Where your mind can only take you the higher.

For today in our lab, we've engineered a new drug
One that makes life an existence of Love.
We offer it to you, today in our hand.
To any and every man woman child in each land.

It's a drug that infects, from one to another.
Spontaneous kindness like that of a mother.
An epidemic of good deeds brought on by our lab
I promise it's the best trip you've ever had.

So take this pill and spread it around,
It won't get you high, you won't feel a sound.
It's nothing you see, a placebo, a fake
The kindness is inside you, you harlot, you rake.

Look inside and find the true inner beauty of friends,
Where peaceful solutions are a means to an end.
Hold hands in the morning, and sing songs in the night
Why use these women to battle and fight.

Tomorrow is dawning, in some place today.
An hour is coming, that has already passed away.
Don't let it be too late, before you take our pill.
Don't let it be too late, before you exert your will.

Authentic Perplexity

Love is an expression, a form of our soul.
Without it depression will soon take it's toll.
Give to your brother, or sister in need.
To my words, pause and take heed.

Let us feed the hungry, and clothe the poor
If we don't have enough, let us grow some more
Instead of paying farmers to let the land rest
Let us grow grain and give it away, wouldn't that be best?

Children are starving, and wasting away.
Did you see American Idol today?
We have so many luxuries we could do without.
But suggest it to some and they scream and shout.

Don't eat meat, some say and others tear flesh
From Mazatlan to Bangladesh
A thousand solutions to all of our woes
A thousand thoughts to keep us on our toes

But the solution is in front of us, all we have to do is see
It's been there all along, for you and for me
Money isn't important, neither are material needs
The road to freedom is paved with good deeds.

Tomorrow morning, when you rise look towards the East
Think of the children while you enjoy your morning feast.
Your ham and your eggs, or your bagel with cheese
Even a glass of orange juice is more than these.

Imagine the starving, the poor and the meek
Just a few calories is all that they seek
While we in our comfort, feast each day
Losing weight is our goal, we must find a way

Let's stop worrying about ourselves, and think about others
Or would you have them die, would that were your druthers?
Think of those children, one every three seconds dead.
Keep that thought around in your head.

Poetry by Brian Mullins

So tomorrow, again look towards the sun.
Before you head out to relax in your fun.
Your golf, your football, your quick game of tag
While your shopping and toting that heavy, laden bag

That for just a few seconds, a prayer, and some money
You can make the whole world the land of milk and honey
So today I ask you, join me in peace and harmony
That hunger and oppression might remain a memory

Authentic Perplexity

inspiration

My Muse is beauty, found in all things
From the curve of the breast, to the birds that sing
The hip of my lover, to the clouds in the sky
The shades of her love, to the depths of her eye

My Muse is the body, female so divine
Each curve a letter, a note so sublime
I find prose in her bosom, and music in her laugh
Full songs are written when I take her to bath

Water cascading, down an exquisite frame
Brings all my words, and my writing to shame
For nothing can express the beauty of her skin
Sometimes I think trying with words is a mortal sin.

Her lips like fountains, to drink from in need
Her neck a pasture to graze from, to feed
The sinful delight that is called her back draws my gaze
Leaving me constantly in a funk, in a daze

So you see my muse is a woman, that none can attain
One who brings me so much pleasure, and so much pain
Her touch is lightning, burning me to the core
Leaving me begging, wanting for more

Her womb is my palace, where life is proclaimed
Where childhood conceived, as God preordained
To nurture and care, and provide with her life
For you see, my Muse is none other than my loving wife.

Poetry by Brian Mullins

an age old question

I sit here sweating.
Wondering why?
Why was I hurt so bad in the past?
What did I do to deserve my wonderful wife?
Why does she love me?
Why do people like what I write?
Why?
It's such a short word, but it means so much.
I am confounded by it on a daily basis.
Why?
Am I alone in this?
Am I the only one who asks why?
Why was war so important to some?
Why did so many die in the name of Church?
Why do some blame all Christians for the same reason?
Why am I concerned at all with what others think?
Why?
Why do I feel crushed inside?
Like someone has beaten me with a baseball bat.
Like a truck backed over me twice, the first time ineffective.
Why?
Why do I get depressed for nothing?
Why do I cry alone, and never show it?
Why do I sleep alone most nights?
Why?

Authentic Perplexity

thunderstorm

The rain calls to my soul like a long lost lover.
One who has always been there, it is I who have severed ties.
It sings to my body, to my heart.
It calls me brother. It calls me sister. It calls me friend.

I want to dance with my lover and let her caress my skin
I want to give in to my childhood memories and forget.
Let the water wash over me like millions of fingers looking for delight.
Watch the lightning illuminate me in a lovers embrace.

Can you feel the clouds watching as we consummate ourselves
Bringing forth wave upon wave of orgasmic froth
Dancing like we are possessed shaking the water from our hair
Caressing ourselves as the rain comes down

Shivering from the cold or the touch, I'm not sure anymore
As my lover drenches my spirit in heavenly fluid
I am spent, cold, but not alone
For the storm continues to hold and caress me long after we are done

Poetry by Brian Mullins

dream scape

If you could see the world in my dreams;
Amidst the orgasms amidst the screams
A artists world trapped behind a pen
No telling who, where, what or when

In kindergarten we are taught to rhyme
Some learn it well, others pantomime
Do your emotions scream off the page?
Hate, love, anger, lust, and rage?

A vision created of love so dear,
A woman of beauty always so near.
A lust for her that I cannot contain
Alas for posterity I must restrain

When you close your eyes and the world reveals
A land of delight, filled with resounding squeals
A world where life itself is a sexual zenith
No one on top, and no one beneath

All are equal and all are perfection
No need for police, no need for protection
A land of dreams, only a breath away
Available to us both night and day

So close your eyes my love, and let the day fall behind
Let your emotions take over, follow your mind.
Give into your fantasies and follow the whispers
Through the glades, the forest, the towering timbers

I'll meet you there you know, on that golden shore
Where we will not wish nor want for more
Surrounded by loved ones, healed of all ills
This world made of love, not of blue little pills

Authentic Perplexity

the shepherd

A shepherd on the mountain top, looks oft for his sheep.
Whether they are grazing, mulling or asleep.
His mindful eye is on them, watching their every move
They've nothing they can hide from him, yet nothing to prove

He guides them slowly, gently, keeping them from harm
Walking slowly at their side, sometimes offering an arm
Ever peering for dangers in the road ahead
Lest one of his precious sheep end up lost or worse, dead

Day after day, he watches and guides his lamb
The faithful, the loving, the angry and the damned
We take for granted something so full of love and free
He just wants what's best for them, can't they see?

But a friend of mine said something that moved me in my core
After seeing that after God's correction, some are angry, mad, or sore.
She said a line that made me think, something that was profound and deep
You see a shepherd uses his crook to guide, but he never harms his sheep

Poetry by Brian Mullins

living in a daze

Fog, stealthy and slow, settles into the crevice of my skull.
It's ninjitsu tactics allow it creep unnoticed until I am in it's control.
My patience a venomous snake, buried under a stone
Striking at innocents, and antagonists alike.
My brackish sprinklers are on again, soaking a mask of granite
Seductive lips in an implacable cast.
Solitary souls accompanied by new formed canvas
Wishing Limbo wasn't so near or far
A wooden chisel, inches from my heart
Notes of pain renewing dismay
Three rivets divert the eye from grain
As unfulfilled consumption surrounds my grave
Capturing the soul of the innocent tribes
Digital imprisonment on a stand
While cartoons dance on a whiskey glass
Expounded verse under woven hair
Previous lovers clothes next to fancy dress
An ornament unlived, a box empty
I am lugubrious made man

Authentic Perplexity

~~time~~

Your time is like a bar of gold,
Weighing down all things around
If only it were like times of old,
Instead alone here I drown.

We once were pirates on the ocean,
Counting our treasure side by side.
Now you keep on sailing unseen,
While I alone sigh and hide

Fields of grain, we would glide
Side by side we ran
Till one day you found your stride
Will I see you again?

In the distance I saw a flicker
A light of hope did spark
Till on the hill a chair of wicker
Was all of your passing mark

So I sit in this chair alone
Till again you pass me by
Stop and sit and sins atone
Sit for once and look me in the eye

Life is passing, life is fleeting
Only a short time have we to go
Do not waste those chance meetings
Cause destiny, you'll never know

Poetry by Brian Mullins

wrong time, wrong place

There was a time, when men lived in harmony with the world
They danced, they sang, they communed with God
They lived amongst the trees, and sang their love of the Earth
Then they came along and killed them

Then there was a man, who believed in peace
He believed in love, and honor, and trust
He lived a life pure of all sin and hate
Then they came along and killed him

There were many of them, living on their grassy lands
Communing with Nature, listening to God and the world
Dancing and singing, one with the land
Then they came along and killed them

There once was a little girl, living on the streets
She could have had a meal, she could have had food
She lived each night shivering and praying for help
They never came along, which killed her

The druids, they danced and honored the land
The Indians, they danced and honored the land
Jesus, he loved and honored all, in the name of his father
You and I, we came along and killed them

It's too late for us, in that aspect.
We cannot travel back in time and learn their secrets.
But we can help her, we can come along.
We can come along.

The animals in the shelters, the ones with no homes.
The children in orphanages or on the streets.
The broken beggar, destroyed protecting our homes
We can come along, that they might live

Authentic Perplexity

even i

Once a lofty goal, to take a crown from on high
Left us to fall to earth, mortal and to die
Darkness was proclaimed of all, once noble and true
Alone to face the realm of waste, and then he made You

To mingle in and out of life, maybe even to merge.
Our hearts with lofty goals, our souls to purge
Forgiveness offered to all, gentile and Jew
He came down here to save, You

Bitterness and anger, fists full of hate
Love is the answer, but for most it is too late
Forgiveness for all, promised by his Son
A battle that we thought was lost, but in the end he won

Can we return to our place aloft, with our friends and foes
Away from this place with it's rains and it's snows
This forbidden garden where nothing blooms and only death awaits
Or are we bound here, is that our fates

You see, there are so many, dwelling in amongst man
Doesn't matter, black or white, green, blue or tan
Love can save us too, Christian, Wiccan, Jew
For I'm more than a man, I'm a fallen angel too

Will you be that angel to lift me up in need
To love me despite your hate, in my time of need?
or will you turn your back, and let me fall on down
In my own pity to wallow, ruminate and drown

Poetry by Brian Mullins

goodbye

a spider, casts its web
fly unaware
tree, spray painted
red X's in the forest
a plunderers treasure
darkness on a sunny day
the bulb of the plant
in feces does rest
steel fingers shredding
sweat falling down
too small that motorcycle
a grill mired in the mud
closing in, panic driven
tools under the snow
weeds poking through
loose fence boards in the wind
a flag fallen to the ground
trash in the brush
food in the floor
shirt too short
alone

Authentic Perplexity

~~epiphany~~

Words of fallacy dance too and fro
As my child not from infancy does grow
Paternal instincts have kicked her in gear
Compulsion to do things year after year

God is in here, and God is in me
We are part of him, and he of us you see
Light dawning in her eyes, comprehension aware
Every time she tells a lie God is right there

Stop here I could, but go on I must
I do not want to lose this ones trust
For I realize that in my own head, does God reside
He's not across the street, he's right here inside

Aware of our innermost, every single thought
When we do what shouldn't, when we do what we ought
When we lie to another, who has God inside
Didn't we in fact just tell him a lie?

Oh how deep that thought did run, a chill down my spine
Cause not only did it dawn in her eyes, it dawned in mine
Down a road of thought I had never before trod
Down a highway I slowly did plod

For if God is inside, and part of me
And I tell a lie, do you see what I see?
My insides burn and tingle with fire
Cause you see when I lie.. I make God a liar

Poetry by Brian Mullins

darkest day

In my drug stupored haze
Reality became a sham
Your puppet your zombie
What you want is what I am

I gave you my heart
An offering on a platter
I never got it back
It still covers the plaster

Love notes on a screen
Floating hearts in ethereal mist
Your last name wasn't mine
All this just a tryst

Ten years of solitude
Walking that line
All this time thinking
I was yours and you were mine

A circle saw in my toolbox
Such a cruel instrument for that
A cut here, incision there
Through sinew and fat

I wanted it you know
To end it all there
I would have too
I know you didn't care

Darkness was my mistress
Now for this time
To enter it forever
Would be so sublime

Authentic Perplexity

*The photos, the vids
All done by me
Something we shared
Something for us to see*

*But you gave to them, to them
And said you made them with your heart
That they were JUST for them
Where does the agony start*

*The dress that I bought you
The one with the flair
Complimented your eyes
Went so well with your hair*

*But you made it a game
Scrabble for fun
Fill in the blank
Hit and Run*

*So in the darkness I sit
With you all alone
Offering you my heart
Agape, your sin to atone*

*"I never loved you"
I remember that's what you said
"I never loved you"
I remember as you turned your head*

*Ten years of marriage
Just flowed down the drain
Ten years of marriage
Sometimes I still feel that pain*

Poetry by Brian Mullins

mindless

Flocks of seagulls
in a turbine engine
mindless drones
for their King bee

Confucius speaks
marbles listen
An arrow at a target
In another lane

Bowling with apples
at concrete pins
Comments of praise
seduction for abuse

Bus loads of fans
screaming their praise
for a rock group of skeletons
propped up on a stage

A name is the bringer
arrogance the key
confounding the message
honesty the disarmer

A garbage truck of sarcasm
loading up at each can
How long do you think
will live an honest man?

Authentic Perplexity

cut and paste

I asked you for a poem
A piece of you in prose
A part of your heart on paper
A part of your soul in graphite
You made me a master piece
Of falsehood and lies
One line from this one
One line from that
A note pasted from magazines
A macabre ransom demand for my core
All you did was cut and paste
Till my heart was on the floor

Poetry by Brian Mullins

reborn

It often hits me like a seizure
an explosion of the mind
my self inflicted cocoon
silk of emotion, strands of fear

Wrapped in my warm hollow
I am safe from the world
cuddling and swaddled
by my own inner soul

Content am I, for a time
till my cocoon begins to dry
constricting, a stalker
a wolf in sheep's clothes

Air is constricted
blocked off by dismay
fighting and struggling
to break free from myself

A cocoon created for safety
for warmth and shelter
is now my downfall
I slowly falter

Despair is my mistress
seducing my ghost
into primordial ooze I descend
no chance or hope

A hand in the darkness
a lighthouse in a monsoon
beckoning for me to swim
urging me forward

She screams in frustration
gripping tighter around my throat
this succubus named gloom
but the hand grasps me and pulls me through

Authentic Perplexity

From my cocoon of depression
I slowly emerge
A reborn spirit
Aloft with the birds

Poetry by Brian Mullins

dewdrops cover...

Dewdrops cover the morning grass
As I look through the drapes at the sky
The haunting melody of the wind
As dewdrops cover my eye

I know that freedom is but a latch away
And a simple flick of the wrist
But the door is made of brick and mortar
The windows of steel, bars that cannot twist

Yesterday was freedom, yesterday was grace
Today is hollow and unfound
Oblivion was pure and absinthe so sweet
Today I yearn for a sound

A bird in a tree, a rabbit in the bush
Echoes of children at play
A car in the street, a plane in the sky
Sorry my friend not today

Dewdrops cover the morning grass
As I look through the drapes at the sky
The haunting melody of the wind
As dewdrops cover my eye

Authentic Perplexity

a joyful noise

*The words are flowing like a crystalline stream,
hardly pausing for me to catch my breath.
They bounce around in my cranium, striving to be free.
I see them dance, and hear their sounds,
tinkling inside like an ice cream truck jingle.
As they pour from my finger tips, they meld on their own
forming their own poem. Their own song. Their own form.
I do not own my write, it owns me. I do not give to my write,
it takes what it needs.
Do you feel the passion that rocks my core?
An avalanche of syllables banging against my spine
Cascading down a muddy terrain of forested growth
To land on shredded trees.
Perhaps they call from their recycled graves,
do the trees inspire us from their spiral bound coffin?
Does hope inspire to display your mind,
an operating table for students to poke and prod.
A heckler in the back, complaining about size and color
The dimensions of the brain are lacking
Make a joyful noise, with your eyes.
Let your ears be your souls refuge
Resonate your breath till the frequency burns
And pour your blood out till our symphony is complete.*

Poetry by Brian Mullins

what are you sorry for?

I am sorry
I am sorry that I don't believe what you believe.
I am sorry that when I read my bible, it doesn't say what you said.
I am sorry that when Jesus tells me to love everyone, that I love homosexuals as well.
I am sorry that when I worship I use a candle, and incense, and pray.
I am sorry that I don't go to Church every Sunday.
I am sorry that sometimes I pray out loud, and it Rhymes.
I am sorry that I believe in Magick.
I am sorry that I would freely worship with a Wiccan Coven as I would with a Catholic or Baptist.
I am sorry that I believe it's ok to heal people through Reiki.
I am sorry that I believe that Hypno therapy is ok.
I am sorry that I believe that everything Good comes from God.
I am sorry that I didn't write this sooner.

But most of all.

I am sorry that you don't understand why I believe the way I do
I am sorry that you don't take the time to listen to what I say before you tell me I'm wrong.
I am sorry that we aren't as close as we used to be, because I believe in Love.
I am sorry that I am not sorry at all.

Authentic Perplexity

oblivion

sweet oblivion
a nothingness escape from reality
i long for emptiness
the dark solace
where time does not exist
silence roaring, a deafening orchestra
sanctuary of the mind
my head a shillelagh
forever tormenting itself
against the banks of Lethe
absinthe i beg of you
just a glass

Poetry by Brian Mullins

the spirit

The spirit she moves me,
Like an all consuming blaze
Burning inside my soul
Guiding me through the days

Touching my inner self
She gives me thoughts to pleasure
Moving my mind to peace
An infinity of treasure

Descending on to self
She lights up my sensations
A lazer show, in the dark
Of paranormal expressions

She gathers wisdom to me
And takes hatred apace
Lifting my senses heavenward
Throughout this inner space

A promise that was given
That man would receive her kiss
If we but accept it
Our lives can be filled with bliss

Our father, the son, the spirit all are near
The father to discipline and love us
The son to make amends
The spirit to fill our minds with wisdom and trust

So when you feel her moving
Up and down your spine
Realize that she is forever there
Wisdom so divine

Authentic Perplexity

untitled

Does your mind grasp the depth of my words?
Or feel the venom of my gaze
Or are you a plexi-glass storm pane
Hidden in your own daze

Past your own Dickenson scheme
Through the field of dreams
Do you skip with mountain tops and rainbows
While the rest of us drown in screams?

What is your purpose here to guide
For everyone is failing in your own eyes
A raging storm, at high tide
Where everyone but his holiness dies

Venom is best doused alone
Fire in your throat does not atone
For glimpses of depth in a one dimensional hole
Your creative energies are gone

Poetry by Brian Mullins

tired

Sluggish
I am Pain
Agony flows through my veins
Tears are my blood
A saline vampire
Cast out for regret
My eyes are cement
My feet oaken roots
Collapsing again
For tomorrow

Authentic Perplexity

message

The universe has a message for each of you my friends,
It's your choice to accept it or ignore it in the end.
Peace and understanding and unity with earth
Not money and expansion, to solidify our girth

So many peaceful solutions, so many ways to correct
The damage we have already done, but peace is called a sect
Arming those against it, and arming those for
Killing God's children in the name of peaceful war

Each of our religions, teaches peace and tolerance
But do you see it in any person, even one instance?
We crucify the homosexuals, and ridicule the few
And then we complain and wonder why we can't fill a pew

Jesus' message was so simple, and had not a single flaw
Love is the answer, the whole of the Law
Love the father, the lord your God, in whatever form you choose
And love your neighbor as yourself what else have you to loose?

If you love your neighbor, as you love yourself
You wouldn't put their friendship in the back of the shelf.
In their time of need, you'd be right there at their side
It wouldn't take your dogma to help you to decide

If your son or daughter told you they were gay,
Would you disown them and send them on their way?
Or would you choose to love them, and realize they are who they are
Cherish and love them, as you would a precious star

The galaxy is in your hands, if only you choose to perceive
This is not a lecture, or an attempt to deceive
We are one, and all are we, one in the divine
You are my friend, and I am yours, together we are mine

Poetry by Brian Mullins

So reach deep down inside, and listen to that still small voice
And realize that man does not control you, you still have a choice
God is speaking to you, and all you need is to hear
He's never far away, actually he's quite near

Forgive your friends and forgive yourself, for ceremony is not of import
It's better to bite your tongue than to snip in retort
Do unto others as they would do unto you
So many rules, but then again so few

Love is the answer, and love is the whole
Love is the reason, the foundation of the soul
Give your love freely and freely it shall return
And for your friends love, you shall never have to yearn

Do what thou wilt, and it harm none
What harm to you has this phrase done
Yet we persecute and call them witch and devil
What did they do wrong, what perceived you that was evil?

The Qu'ran, the Torah, the Bible, Book of Mormon or book of Light,
Why let the question of which is right keep you up at night?
Just let the Spirit guide your mind, and study to show yourself approved
Then if it is God's will, your soul and mind shall be moved

Reach out your hand to the downtrodden, the persecuted and beat
Feed the hungry, love the children, and help to wash their feet
For when you show love, you honor God in the only way he asks
And he will show you the way to perform his will and do his holy tasks

Life is too short for hatred, ridicule and shame
Ghandi didn't hurt you, he isn't the one to blame
Muslims aren't all evil, not everyone is involved
The spirit can divine wrong, mysteries can be solved

Open your mind's eye, and let God do the seeing
It will keep you from jerking your knee and instantly fleeing
For every person is different, every person can be Love
Why do you think the Spirit descended like a dove?

Authentic Perplexity

A sign to unbelievers that God's love was pure
A sign to believers, so their faith to ensure
So this message the spirit sends, and he does persist
That we can in love and peacefully equally coexist.

Namaste

Poetry by Brian Mullins

midnight confessions

As I child I watched from the window sill,
As he silently passed by on his trek in the stars
His rays washing over me, caressing me,
Past constellations, planets, Venus, then Mars

The gentle faces flowing, from happy to sad
Waxing and waning, he came and disappeared
Always above even when I couldn't see
I could sense when he was near

My totem does call and to it I beckon
The heart of a wolf, crying to be let free
Gently he listened to my confessions
As I realized the one crying was always me

Now that I'm older, the voice is dim
But the call is there to come confess my sin
A long awaited friend alone in the night
The wolf calling softly, my soul mate, my twin

The summer heat wafting, and breezing through
My bare skin rippling, shimmering in the night
I step to my window, naked in my glory
My heart clinched in my chest, my eyes close tight

To the moon, my friend, my lover
I confess my heart, my soul, my tears
He listens gently still in the moist night air
And with his light washes away all my fears

Authentic Perplexity

foot massage

My hands on your canvas flesh
A work of art to mold
Nothing left to perfect
I'd never be so bold

My fingers as troubadours
Writing out their song
To touch in such a way
I have wanted for so long

A moment of passion
Locked in your gaze
A moment forever
Mind in a daze

Your pulse, rapid
Through your heel
Raised flesh rising
As I kneel

Scent of forbidden
On the air
Hands moving slowly
Ever there

A sensual seduction
Of lingering means
How can my mind
Comprehend these things

Poetry by Brian Mullins

~~men~~

when is a man good enough
when can he deserve
the love of a woman
how can he have the nerve

when a pedestal for her he builds
and on it she comfortably rests
and nothing does he ask of her
no hidden agenda, no tests

if from this pedestal she does fall
catching her is his duty
placing her back on it
kissing her bruises his bounty

when her feet ache from a long day
a massage for them alone
rubbing with no ulterior motive
no sins to later atone

her shoulders a rising dough to knead
just because they're there
pushing and folding, and making whole
removing all pockets of air

her hips a trembling sigh on his lips
to touch and cherish at will
her hand to his lips to kiss
while prostrate and contrite he does kneel

her arms to trace with love
slowly with one trembling finger
careful not to wake her in her sleep
while on her lips he does linger

Authentic Perplexity

dinner to cook with joy and zeal
as often as one can
this I tell you is the ultimate joy
that passion of a true man

to know your love is nourished
and filled to the brim with passion
this is not the world of yesterday
cooking is in fashion

so when does a man truly deserve
the woman of his dreams?
he doesn't and he probably won't
but to her he does stream

and through her grace
she loves him flaws and all
and they in turn from time to time
catch each other when they fall

Poetry by Brian Mullins

thorn

You are a thorn in my side
With each step that I take
Though I should forgive
You teach me to hate

Like a razor in my shoe
You make my feet bleed
Never there to help
Only there to need

You don't ask you take
You never offer to give
Not even for their sake
Only for your endless sieve

Your mind is a gutter
Your life a waste
What I wouldn't give for revenge
Even a taste

I promised I won't
Make you disappear
I promised I won't
Even interfere

But be glad for those words
Which I will not take back
For without them I'd probably
Bound and attack

You deserve it you know
You sick son of a bitch
To be beaten to a pulp
And left in a ditch

Authentic Perplexity

Playing mind games with young girls
Making them think it's their own choice
But what your really doing
Is crushing their inner voice

Go away is all I ask
And leave us alone
Let us be a family
Just a happy home

Poetry by Brian Mullins

friends

A flower grew, out behind the house
One of rare beauty and grace
It touched my heart, and made me love
Though I had never seen her face

So I tended the soil, and nourished the ground
Of which we both relied
So that she could flourish though far away
Though both our hands were tied

Oft she disappeared, and went away
For months, years at a time without heed
But always she bloomed and sprouted
Right when I had a need

Just when things were rough and I needed a friend
I'd find her in the oddest place
A flower blooming in the street, a cantina or forest
But always right before my face

Then one day our bond were free
Our roots were pulled up from the soil
So travel I did from place to place
Doing my traveling toil

Then one day where did I find myself to be
But in the garden of her choice
I traveled six hundred miles to see
That she was more than just a voice

Now two flowers grow, in the garden behind the house
Along with four sprouts, who they love so
So if your flower is far away, and free of any roots
Then do no tarry, do not stray, simply go

Authentic Perplexity

what am i?

The words flow like sap, in and out of the cracks of a maple tree.
Their meaning lost on a roaring deaf crowd
My eyes filled with a saltine river flowing over a monotonous terrain
A nest of spider eggs filling my throat, their cotton blocking all sound

I am a tree in the wilderness, falling so that one man might pose a question
A butterfly on the wind, spreading pollen for a plant who doesn't care
My mind a dream catcher, parsing nightmares like an aged computer
Slowly analyzing, never fast enough for my liking

I am a weed in the garden of life, looking to strangle the other plants
Choking them back with my mediocrity, never good enough for my own genus
A fleeting rainbow, fading long before any one can view with the eyes of a child
A dry land fish, before a rain storm. Unseen. Unknown. Ready to bloom into my own ugliness.

Why then am I inspired to pass along what little I glean?
Why must I put to words those thoughts that others dare not speak?
Why must I feel those emotions that others want to hide?
Because I must.

Poetry by Brian Mullins

the greatest dishwasher of all

The dishwasher clogged up earlier.
I had to clean the trap out by hand
Slowly pulling pieces of lettuce, carrot, unidentifiable meats
All from water that I could not see through
A veil that kept my eyes from seeing what was going on
It reminded me of our daily lives
How they are so full of junk
Things that rot and fill our days
How we have so many things in this little traps in our minds
That we just don't let go of
A piece of a relationship here
A piece of a heartbreak there
Two strands of long forgotten lust

Then I realized that Jesus was like that filter
in the bottom of my dishwasher
He filters out the filth, and holds it at bay
Sometimes it backs up and we just need to let it all go
So that he can keep washing us clean

Authentic Perplexity

writing

A dove lands on a tree limb
Seeking shelter from a storm
Not because this tree is special
But because it is the norm

For if he could not find this tree
he'd quickly be blown away
For the storm rages whether the dove wants or not
causing even the heartiest to sway

An alligator in it's bed, resting from a full course meal
Waiting for the young to feed, with fervency and zeal
It's mind groggy, with the feeling of content
Not caring that it's mate is near nor of his intent

Awaking and staggering through, this crocodile of fear
Seeing the nest it's mate has made, doesn't shed a tear
Instead it turns and saunters off, to find more to shred
While it's mate is there alone, mind filled with dread

A flower in the garden grows, turning towards the sun
It's mind filled with laughter and hope, joy and fun
Growing slowly, each day for to spread it's seed
It's lilting song, it's heavenly scent, it's only need

But then the farmer comes along, and plucks it from the ground
Ignoring it's protests, not caring for it's sound.
So to this end the beauty has come, to be ignored
Can this beauty ever be enjoyed, can she be implored

Poetry by Brian Mullins

in the dark

I remember how you moved
A belly dancer astride
Hips alive like water at high tide
My mind riveted to yours
Souls intertwined
A river of Eden flowing
While the moon danced high above
Sultry music on a clock radio
Scent of musk heavy in the air
Your hair alive and swirling
Anemone in the wind
Your breasts two fine jewels
Turgid and erect
Your stomach a divine stretch of flesh
My tongue a dancing minstrel
Traveling in a land of lust
Looking for the Llano
Finding the crevice of your lust
Does your mind explode
Do you lose control?

I remember how you moved
In the Dark

Authentic Perplexity

flight of the damned

Escape this hell I must, before it consumes me
This barren wasteland, where nothing grows
I shall craft a bird to carry me aloft
To a place that no one knows

Run after me if you wish, but catch me you won't
Warden of this hells domain
For your feet cannot lope fast enough
To catch this leaving train

This fog ahead, doth inspire fear
But forge on I must
For to stay in this forgotten place
Will only destroy my trust

My mind protests, and claims it can't be done
For flight has never been achieved
But if I stay here, my life will end
How will that be perceived?

So aloft I go, in flight for free
To a land where the grass is green
I shall soar, through the fog and mists
And anything in between

Poetry by Brian Mullins

discarded

A discarded monkey
on a cold concrete slab
eerie how it's eyes seemed to follow me
I could have picked it up and put it away
But it seemed wrong to disturb it's funeral
Others had gathered you see
Nearby to watch the monkey
Who showed no signs of performing
He wasn't going to ride a unicycle
or dance for peanuts.
He had simply been discarded
Do you think he felt it, when from her fingers he slipped?
To be left on the cold, hard, man made slab
To sleep the night alone
With no friends in sight
Just the barbies, mocking because he's not as good as they are
The leggos, disjointed and out of place, not aware of anyone else
The kitchen set, with stains from a hard life
The trash bag, which is where all the bad toys go
Do you think he knows?
Or is he just a monkey
On a cold man made slab?

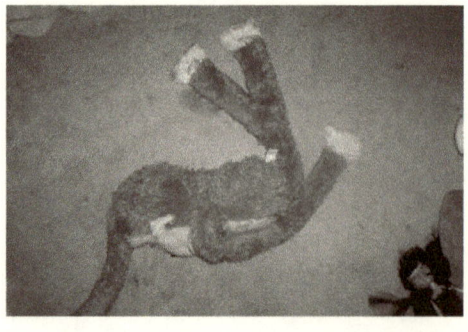

Authentic Perplexity

a mirror

As I gaze into reflections of a world that should be,
I can't help but wonder, if the man looking back is even me,
A writer, a poet, electrician, bus driver, pizza short order cook,
His outlook changes with every look

Behind him images flutter, doubts and despair
As I notice it's time again to cut off my hair
A fleeting memory here, a fading image there
Can I find my way from here, but to where?

Did I make my parents proud, or let them down again
Did I earn my way to heaven, or drown myself in sin
Will I make my fortune writing or fall down on my face
Am I where I ought to be, is this my only place

My eyes are ringed and deepened, pools of darkened life
Filled with night terrors and fears, anger, and strife
My mouth a permanent smile, or so I have been told
I used to be so prominent, standing out, serious, bold

But here I am, this semi attractive man, hiding behind a wall
Scared of the slightest sound, so insignificantly tall
But in the mirror I also see a glimmer of light
Keep trying it seems to say, and everything will be alright

Poetry by Brian Mullins

sometimes

Sometimes I watch you sleep
is that creepy?
I watch as you breath in and out
your bosom rising with each zephyr
carrying your scent throughout my existence
the angry fingers of your hair grasping,
clutching at the pillow case
an epic battle of satin versus flame
eyes dancing to an unknown vision
sighing, perhaps moaning,
and unknown lover in your dreams
sometimes I'm jealous of him
ethereal supplications, suppositions
other times your presence is as the sun
warming me on a cold winter morning
my face tingling as fingers of light caress my cheeks
forcing me to snuggle even deeper into you
I am reduced to a babe
snuggling for warmth
nuzzling for suck

Authentic Perplexity

blood boils

did you not see that you held a pearl?
a gift from god in your hands,
lustrous and full of life
glimmering in the sunlight
for all to see, a gift so sincere
can not be bought
nor can it be battered or beaten
into submission
it must be earned
or it's not a gift
you see you took a pearl
which you could have cherished
shown your family
your friends
instead you made it a necklace
you pierced it and tucked it away
absentmindedly you'd chew it when angry
and mark it with your teeth
now scratched, battered, and broken
you toss it to the side, and look for another
one flaw in your plan
there are those of us who see
the pearl you tossed aside
and we pick them up
we dust them off
we polish them and cherish them
nourish and heal them
make them whole again
and we teach them
that you are slime
that your kind don't deserve a pearl
your kind don't deserve to breathe

Poetry by Brian Mullins

we danced

The tunnel seemed closed, and far away
But my eyes were deceiving me
For things that had crumbled, were secreted afar
And simply out of my sight to see

The demons had relinquished their grasp
And my feet were finally free
To stride a drum line beat
From the darkness to flee

The pathway, foreboding and grim
Paved with leaves of yore
Ancient runes lined the stones
Long forgotten lore

In the light my nymph I did see
From flower, to stream she pranced
A roe, into her arms I bound
And the sun rose as we danced

Authentic Perplexity

i taste you

My Lord has called, to him I serve
The ring it calls, death you deserve
I taste your scent, on the night air
Your filthy sweat, from you I tear

My mind it feels, the rings cry
To leech your soul, to make you die
Your finger you think, it to place
The air trembles around, to you I trace

I sense your soul, I sense your need
Find you I must, find you I plead
But a hand of a friend, calls you back
With his support I quickly lose track

Find you again, that I do swear
Your body to rip, your flesh to tear
I will suck out your soul, and make you weep
Sending your corpse to the vasty deep

Poetry by Brian Mullins

voice of a siren

Your lips call to me
A siren in a wasteland
Luring me towards the shore
That I might crash into your ocean

I consume you
A forborne sailor in need of sustenance
I taste your scent, meld your tongue
Oblivion takes my mind

I am a heartbeat
A pulse in a vein
Throbbing, immersed in your fragrance
Your aroma fills my soul

You pull back for air
Your neck exposed
A cornucopia of flesh
A superfluity of sensuality

The clock is ticking
You must abscond
Your body moistened
Your mind afloat

Pushing yourself away
I beg for more
Later my love
Our Rendezvous

Authentic Perplexity

to the deep

A wonderful trip I had always planned
to see the world from the sea
a bow of a boat or from an island shore
seemed such a thrill to me

A submarine to carry me down
to see the ocean floor
I never thought that I would be
knocking on Poseidon's door

This ocean whose depths I now explore
is found only for me
an ocean of filth, mire and muck
an ocean only I see

An ocean who sucks the very life
straight from the marrow of your bone
a razor's edge so very sharp
not even the most skilled can hone

reaching out my hand I seek relief
from this grave at sea
but it's only the moon, the sky, the water
my depression and me

Poetry by Brian Mullins

my phantoms

darkness surrounds me
taking my breath away
an ethereal chill
filling me to my core
my soul
trying to wrench it from me
no one can take that
but they try
creek and crack
laughter in an empty room
running down the hall
no one there
a toilet flushing itself
possessed
alone
calling out
no one hears
mind wandering
eyes closed
imagining despair
living distraught
minds eye focused
seeing things not to be seen
meditation
clears nothing
concentrate
numb
alone

Authentic Perplexity

waking

I heard a sound of joy
echoing through my skull
a coo of sheer delight
out of sleep it did lull

A bundle of laughter
from a package so small
smiling a toothless grin
made me feel ten feet tall

Humming and laughing
at lifeless cotton facsimiles
shaking her fists and feet
not sure if friends or enemies

her raven black hair
my snow white in swaddling
I love to watch her crawl
can't wait to see her waddling

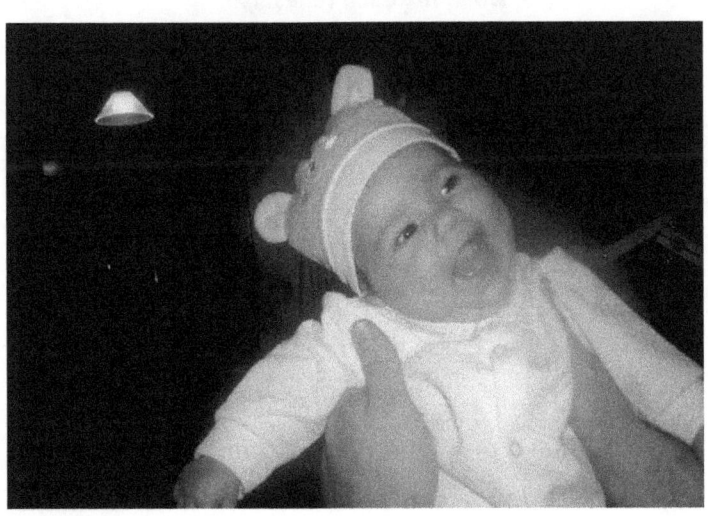

Poetry by Brian Mullins

falling

i saw my eye fall today
a moment of discordant harmony
from ecstatic joy was the top of my rise
down a slope to steep to walk
stumbling rapidly lest i trip and slide
stirring up the sand of my wasteland
while the hollow of me stood at the top
laughing for my despair
was it a funny thing to watch
a slow motion decent amidst a cloud of Fae
hating the inner workings of my mind
while the outer smiled onward
confusion
a word with meaning
counterclockwise movement of my second hand
reliving passion while passion abounds
a defunct guitar, with broken strings
unable to play a chord
while the band tunes up
my notes blow hollow

Authentic Perplexity

the scent

Across the room I move, slowly, exquisite pain
I can smell that which is you, a flower in the rain
I feel your heartbeat shudder through the air
I see your throat tighten, suddenly aware

Did you know I can taste you, floating through my mind
That I can feel you, touching, caressing, moments in time
I see your pulse throb, in your long sensuous throat
Now to cross your boundaries, your moat

A bead of sweat, betrays your mood
As I lower my cloak, my cowl, my hood
Towards you I pounce, one step at time
Knowing without a doubt that I will make you mine

To the wall I pin your hands, your mouth I consume
The moans of delight rise up to the moon
The scent of your loins, filling my core
Every ounce of my being begging for more

Rest you will find is in short supply
A shudder, a twitch, a contented sigh
Yet anew, aflutter, a scent in the sky
And again, there it is, that twinkle in my eye

Poetry by Brian Mullins

this road

This road I walk, I walk alone
A dreary land, within a home
Oft I find, a sign here or there
Distance to someplace much more fair

But I dredge on, my stubborn fate
Hoping to turn before it's too late
For this road has hope, that she planted here
A maiden beautiful, strong with no fear

On my crutch I stumble, unable to walk alone
Fear that I"ll lose myself, chilled to the bone
Trees passing, turning, calling and clinging
Before they were beautiful, chanting and singing

Now dark and twisted, pulling and ripping
Faces gnashing, sharp teeth snipping
Their eyes haunted, their bark decayed
Their twisted sharp fingers, daggers displayed

A light up ahead, my freedom at last
All it would take, is one last dash
Pulling for all my energy, I head for hope
Staggering, falling as I reach the slope

One more step, one more stagger, one more limping despair
Then I could taste it, smell it, feel the fresh air
But again, I stop dead in my tread
My heart filled with fear, filled with deep dread

One more victim to the forest, has fallen today
Lost of their own accord, never finding their way
Why can't they listen, to the wisp of their life
Why must they contain to force their own strife

Authentic Perplexity

Tomorrow they promise, just not today
I will make it from this forest, but in my own stay
For though you guide me and offer me peace
To be my conscience, my soul police

I am not ready to walk on my own two feet
I am not ready to perform this great feat
So my crutch I will cradle, and stumble along
Until my heart sings a victory song

RIVULET IN SHORT LITHE.

Poetry by Brian Mullins

vampire amongst

a rainbow of smoke filled my eye
as the world passed me by
unnoticed, unloved, in a world of art
a fallen angel with a frozen heart

eyes a cold glass, frosty and clear
cheeks slightly rosy, mouth a sneer
hair a storm of icicles, wild and alive
sexual desire my only drive

back to my lair, to seduce and use
your body my canvas, my creation my muse
your blood my feeding, my life, my pain
your corpse all that's left after the drain

a picture of perfection, your lifeless shell
as back to my self, back to my hell
checks once again rosy and eyes full of fire
until the need to feed again, what irony, white ire

into my coffin, slowly I descend
content and sedate, alive in pretend
one of many fallen angels, of which man is myopic
making me the girl next door, and my dinner my pick

Authentic Perplexity

a tree often stands alone

Transfigured in my own mortal coil
Atop this hill I stand, watching over man
Roots dug into tainted soil
I often wonder how they can

Oft their young dance around in spring
And lean on me for my precious shade
Yet they think no little thing
When their paper of me is made

For a thousand years I have stood and seen
The inner and outer workings of man
Never more disappointed have I been
In their inward thinking plan

God gave them dominion over the land
To protect and keep it hale
To work and guide with their hand
Not to whither and make pale

Next time you think to chop me down
Or one of my ilk or kin
Say a blessing from your crown
Before my death you begin

For from all of us does life sustain
for your energy reserves we supply
the world you need to maintain
for without it, we all will surely die

Poetry by Brian Mullins

confession of a slave

you don't have to hate me, i do that for myself
i seethe and loathe and hurt and feed
i don't need your pity either, that i can do without
there is only one thing from you i need

your touch like a candle, melting slowly and sure
making my skin crawl, unable to move
flowing down slowly like honey on a jar
something you know you'd never approve

yearning to explode, a dandelion in the wind
arching and moaning, sounds of sin
avoiding your eyes, avoiding your touch
deep inside i know i can't win

my blood boiling, flowing to the top
my heart not involved this time at all
begging and pleading for it to be done
banging my head against the wall

i don't want this, i don't need this
how can you force me so
a man can't be raped can he?
why do I feel so low?

finished, completed, devoid of anything
my body shriveled and withdrawn
i wait silently in my cell
dreading another dawn

Authentic Perplexity

a plexiglas window

The darkness overcomes me, confined in my space
A Plexiglas window, inches from my face
The moon, a tree branch, clouds up above
Walls of dirt, an empty grave, dug with sweet love

Panic, fear, anxiety, all begin to set in
My life passes before me, my benevolence, my sin
Dirt falling down, a rain of contempt
From this fate I shall not be exempt

I pray for forgiveness, I pray to my God
Another thump, a scattered dirt clod
I see a shadow, a dark form in the night
Features unknown in the eerie moonlight

I scream and I plead, don't leave me to die
I did nothing to you, who are you? Who am I?
A glimpse of his face, and finally I see
The man with the shovel, is no other than me

Poetry by Brian Mullins

tears of a geisha

My mask hides my inner turmoil
my makeup a buffer from the universe
to prevent you from getting to close
I know it just makes it worse

How can I tell you how I feel?
if everything is just my crutch
can't you understand that some of us are weak?
some of us can only take so much?

I know your strong and need so little
And can survive on a few minutes a day
I just never dreamed that I would have
to also nourish myself this way

So my pills I diligently take
one at a time, day by day
To slowly make me easier to handle
and erode myself away

Authentic Perplexity

walk with your anchor

Unsteady, an ice floe underfoot
Constantly shifting, changing
Dancing left to right
A constant battle for balance

Fissures form, expand and contract
Covered with the soft powder of deceit
Hidden dangers appearing safe
Waiting for me to fall to my demise

One misstep and down I slide
Ice jagged and sharp
Ripping, slicing, tearing
Stealing life blood of the soul

My anchor just in reach
Comforting me, dragging me forth
Binding my wounds and putting me back on track
Till I might chance to stumble again

Poetry by Brian Mullins

an empty cage

I saw her again today
The girl with the golden locks
I tried to draw her attention my way
Towards this section of the blocks

She smiled her friendly smile
As she went on her way
Promising to come back in a while
Sometime latter today

I laughed inside, how could she know
She was still but a child
That this facade was just a show
Our treatment not so mild

So I wonder as the poison does seep
Tomorrow as she passes her jolly path
Will she stop and gently weep
Or even do the math

Authentic Perplexity

shoveling snow

Today I traversed the divide
Over the chasm I sprawled
One foot on this side
The other in the air, dangling

Demons flew by
their metal bodies salted and fouled
filled with nightmares and dreams
Unaware of my fear

Plunging my tool of destruction
into the white, virgin drift
determined to finished defiling
before retreating from the edge

Feet numb and shriveled
face a ripe plum
black and tan exposed
surrounded by raped goods

Staggering back to my safety
fleeing from freedom to pain
returning, away from liberation
to where I am the most sane

Poetry by Brian Mullins

through the window

I thought I saw the sun today
Dancing alone in my azure sky
I chanced to go out and play
Then fear captured me and I cried

I stood and peered out my window
A glimpse of life before I die
In the distance a golden roe
Taunting freedom if only to try

The clouds so blue and filled with life
To wonder aloud who am I?
To struggle and live with such strife
Then I knew it was just a lie

I thought I saw the sun today
Then fear captured me and I cried

Authentic Perplexity

living in darkness

Altruistic, though my motive may be
Behind the door of my sanity
Calling out to all who can hear
Dreaming of a day I fear
Enthusiasm fills my veins
Forgetfulness, writhes and strains
Good intentions fall to the way
Hell flares up and sours the day
Ignorance of all that I wish to know
Justified in my own inner glow
Knowledge of all that shouldn't be known
Laughing, lying, cheating, only half grown
Mercy I plead and beg and chant
Nothing is responded, go on I can't
Obstinate, a mule standing my ground
Purposely forcing each step, hearing no sound
Quickly I shuffle, a zombie alive
Rarely does life so violently strive
Surely to go on will be easier again
Trying so valiantly to forgive my own sin
Until death do us part, I so did swear
Verily I say, I will always be aware
Whether weary or tired or spent shall I be
Xysteric your love, always to me
Your love is what I have to anchor me here
Zealous for you, my heart sheds a tear

Poetry by Brian Mullins

what the future holds

song lyrics

We've been down that lonely road
And we've both been hurt before
The sky is the darkest
When you can't love no more

Then someone comes along
A friend in need,
And turns your life around,
A friend indeed

I don't know what the future holds,
All I know is the past is gone, and I hold my head up high
I live my life from day to day, waiting for your call
I don't know what the future holds,
But I'm willing to wait and find

I once thought I knew true love
But it was only one way
My heart fluttered like a dove
On my wedding day

Then to find, that she was gone
I didn't know what to do
I was lonesome, all alone,
And who'd I find but you

Theres no one out there like you,
No one to take your place,
I don't know what I would do,
If I'd never seen your face

Authentic Perplexity

For the future for once looks bright,
And the past is really dim
I try to forget her,
And you try to forget him

I don't know what the future holds,
All I know is the past is gone, and I hold my head up high
I live my life from day to day, waiting for your call
I don't know what the future holds,
But I'm willing to wait and find

Friends forever, we will always be
And the future is looking bright
I don't know what the future holds,
But I can feel that this is right.

Things I could never say, and things I couldn't do,
You bring out the best in me, and I often think of you
But the ache I feel inside my chest, dulls each and every day
As you fill my heart with joy, and my brain with images too

I don't know what the future holds,
All I know is the past is gone, and I hold my head up high
I live my life from day to day, waiting for your call
I don't know what the future holds,
But I'm willing to wait and find

Poetry by Brian Mullins

sleep

i thought this morning would be different
i would awaken refreshed and ready to go
i staggered to the window, unable yet to function
to stare at the new fallen snow

something inside me made me believe
that a night of rest would repair
all those mornings of desperate thoughts
of depression and despair

but this morning is the same as all the others
though so much to be thankful for
i still can't venture forth into the world
i still can't open that door

Authentic Perplexity

talent

Shriveled and drowning
In a world of beauty and grace
Writing drivel, writing filth
Pretending to be something

An empty shell
Filling itself with falsehood
An ugly girl in a brown dress
With braces and glasses
Eyes darting back and forth
Just wanting him to see

Where does it end
Or where does it begin
Do I have it?
Did I have it?
Will I have it?

Poetry by Brian Mullins

alone

So I told you, go and have your fun
I wanted to go with you, did you know?
I contemplated it for hours, as I prepared your entourage
Getting together this and that, so that you can make haste and go

How excited they were to have a surprise
A hidden treasure, not knowing what it was but slavering
Pavlov would have been proud of their dancing
I watched as they embarked, no one waving

Did you see me in the window, as I stood till you were gone?
Wanting so much to be there with you, but not to go at all
So I walk the rooms, looking at every sign
Standing alone, facing a wall

Darkness is coming, and no one returned
Closing the casket, my face inches from the wood
Seeking guidance, prayer, and meditation
Wanting to peer outside, wishing I could

Authentic Perplexity

words cannot express

Sometimes I say things, that make me cringe
before I can stop myself they are out, and circling
vultures waiting to dive in and eat the roadkill
that I have just plowed over with my words

An apology doesn't seem enough,
words floating in the air, an unused life preserver
thrown over the side of a sinking boat
For someone who has long since swam to shore

How do I tell you how I feel inside?
The words do not come on their own,
when they do they betray me
vying for their own pardon from the warden

Mayhap I can express in writing
what I cannot express in vocalization
So an apology I send to you from my heart
One that I feel with my soul

I love you

Poetry by Brian Mullins

hunger

Your words fuel my mind
Inspiring my tongue
Flickering in and out
A flame of wish
A flame of dream

Vivid recollections
Of events that have never been
Emotions flowing freely
Desire rampant and apparent

Fleeting fancies and thoughts
Fill the moments
While words and images
Fill the mind
Feed the flame

My mind traces each line
Each part and tremble
Moving slowly, lecherously
From top to bottom
Left to right

Authentic Perplexity

Sighing in contemplation
My mind spent, tired
Inspired again to write
Words that spoken do not

Poetry by Brian Mullins

silent contemplation

Anticipation
Fear
Kneeling, a beaten dog
Shuddering, hiding, cowering
Can he see?

One answer
He does
Sweat, rolling down
Cascading mists, a broken waterfall
Forgiveness, guaranteed, but not accepted

My closet
Secret, hidden
Prayer for my lord, prayer for me
Intimate, foreboding, sensual
Does anyone understand?

Venturing forth
A Sunday ritual
Kindness in asking
Though the answer is obvious
She can't give up on me

Authentic Perplexity

People
Surrounding an alter
Falsehoods, abominations, lies
None there for the reasons
Only there for the hopes

Alone
Drenched in my own salt rain storm
Praying my own pitiful prayers
Hoping that he understands
Knowing
Reflections of My Inner Self

Poetry by Brian Mullins

the ghost

I saw her, standing before me
I'm sure of it.   There she was
glowering back at me for the
things I had done to her.

Of all the things to despise me for
Of all the things to hate me for
She has no right, it's my body to do with as I choose
I don't have to answer to her

Then why is she here?
To torture and torment me?
I must have an answer
I MUST HAVE AN ANSWER

What is this? A snap of a twig?
No she can't be here, she must be inside
She cannot be here to confront me
She must remain where she is

I am in control not her
This is not her body it's mine
Go away I scream but it's too late
She's out, and I'm in

Authentic Perplexity

Trapped inside myself
Unable to fight back
I am losing a fight I did not start
A fight I cannot win

My only hope is when she looks
my way, that she sees me inside.
Cursing and clawing, biting and fighting
working my way slowly to the surface.

Does she fear me as I once feared her?
Or does she know I'm in my place
Maybe that was it all along.
Maybe I am in my place
My place

Poetry by Brian Mullins

the door

It stands there
Taunting me
Knowing that through it lies life
All I have to do is open it
And venture out

Petrified
Unable to move
I want to go, see the Sun
To run and play
To do the things of childhood

Fear courses through me
I am unable to go
My anchor with me I can venture forth
But she's not able
Today she must stay
But I must go alone

One step at a time
I kid myself
You're a man, you can't be scared of anything
You're big, strong, the alpha male
Bark in the face of adversity
Bark like Tarzan, swing on your vine

Authentic Perplexity

But it isn't here
It's not inside of me
I'm not the alpha
Nor the omega
I'm not even the beta

Is it manly to be afraid?
Manly to cry alone in the dark?
Manly to wait for provision from your mate
Will it be dictated by the dregs of society?
Or will we define our own rules?
Our own way of life?

My anchor
She gives me strength
Does she know she is my mainstay?
She is my one and true way of life?
Without her I am afloat in a sea of fear
Afloat in a sea of mankind
Afloat.. alone

Poetry by Brian Mullins

a facade

Often I wonder
About the wiles of this world
The attraction that reels
To a facade in a box
A picture in front
Lures them in
Makes them return

Would it make a difference?
Would more come to peruse?
What if I were one of those
The immaculate falsehoods
Portraying myself in flesh
For words to abound

Many have talent
And many show themselves to be true
Mayhap just jealousy?
Mayhap just fear?
Mayhap

But to remain true
to remain
True

Authentic Perplexity

past

Do you remember
That old brown rug
The one you tried to take me on
How we fought
You in your black dress
Hiked up over your knees
Pushing me to the ground
Trying to take it from me

How your panties clung
And you smelled of desire
But I refused
It wasn't right
Not there
Not just us
Do you remember?

How your tongue tasted
Of stale Marlboro's and Dr. Pepper
A taste I still remember and enjoy
One that I once longed for but no more
The way your bosom heaved
And your dress cleaved
Do you remember?

Poetry by Brian Mullins

The night it happened
In the dark all three?
How we loved each other
Kissing, swapping, tasting
Just the three of us
None wanting
All wanting
None sure
All sure
Do you remember?

Not speaking to me again
Your new boyfriend saying I forced you
Her saying we shouldn't have
Me thinking it would have been ok
No one thinking
All thinking
No one sure
All sure
Do you remember?

Late at night sometimes
Dreaming of this dance
Thinking fondly of what happened

Authentic Perplexity

Never Sorry
Always Sorry
never thinking
Always thinking

I remember

Poetry by Brian Mullins

the invisible man

I stand back in the crowd
Listening to what is happening
Preparing myself for the performance
Waiting for the spotlight
Where she glows like a rose
Lifting her head up, full of pride
Speaking angelically in her funny soprano
Joy fills me inside at such a sight
Then it's over and she runs to hug
Those who made her, and I stand back
I am the invisible man

It's time for her first date
Excitement fills the air
Cutting it in the kitchen with a knife
Fixing her something cold to drink
Laughing at her stories
The ones she's not telling me
The ones I am over hearing
While I make sure she's comfortable
While I make sure everything is ready
She gets ready for her date
And leaves to experience all that life offers
Returning late at night

Authentic Perplexity

Talking all night and calling him
The one who hears it all
The one whom she is always proud of
The one whose libations she enjoys
And I sit by drinking my tea
I am the invisible man

Graduation comes and goes
and life moves on
her husband is nice
But he isn't always so kind
Sometimes he's mean
He gets a call
And he stops being so mean
She comes to talk to her mom
Wondering why he stopped
Glad he did
I stand by listening contently
I am the invisible man

Time continues and life goes on
We solve problems, we make calls
We dance in silence, and sing in empty rooms
We sorrow we experience we live
But no one can see us
We are invisible men

Poetry by Brian Mullins

burning

Burning, I see red
Your heart is filled with ice
Suffer cold one, and live with dread
Do not look to me for sympathy

Do you think it funny, when you laugh?
Or is it your own insecurity showing through?
Do you know how much he cries?
How he has red eyes all morning too?

How heartless and cold can one person be
When a child is needing your touch?
All he asks is for you to love him
Can you deny a child so beautiful this much?

God gives a gift to each and all
And you throw it away
Left over salad, a piece of toast
Just another thing in the trash today

You take your body a temple to God
And you defile and desecrate it in the worst way
You let someone destroy the life inside
A pitchfork seeking for a needle in hay

Authentic Perplexity

Does your mind not see the colors of the sun?
The morning and the clouds, and the rain?
How his hand reaches out and latches on
Holding the hand that inflicts the pain

The hollow sucking, the thud and crush
And the deed is done again
How can you live with yourself
This is beyond just mortal sin

God forgives and people forget
But one day you'll have to realize
That eventually you'll come face to face
With the child that inside you died

Poetry by Brian Mullins

~deflated thoughts~

Dry
Empty
Flailing

Lost
Angry
Turbulent

Emulated
Distraught

Trapped
Horrified
Oscillating

Ungrateful
Grating
Hubris

Tomorrow
Surely

Authentic Perplexity

are we two or one?

Did you feel the same, when we thought of dancing?
Or was it different for you? Was it confusing?
I want to understand all about you, and what makes you move
I want to exscind the past, and explore the future

My heart sighs with content, when I see your face
My body sighs with relief, when you arrive again
Do you hear my soul yearn when you are gone?
Or is it a call that only I feel, when I'm alone?

Your happiness is my desire, my one true calling
So give me the list, the clipboard, the schedule
Tell me how and where, why and what, who and when
I am not good at guessing, not good at figuring

Does confusion set in when you hear my words?
Does satisfaction set in when you see my deeds?
Help me to understand, to cope, to deal
Help me to find, fulfill and cultivate your needs

Poetry by Brian Mullins

tired

2 am
awake again
listening

love
joy
frustration

Happiness
regret
consternation.

Did you think it would be easy?
Did you think it would be fun?
Maybe

Do you regret?
Do you want it to end?
never

Cat naps make up the day,
Micro naps make up the night
Happiness shows you the way,
Ushered by morning light.

Authentic Perplexity

Wishing for Tinkerbell,
and a trip to never-never land
Instead dingy, and bedraggled
Soiled and in your hand.

Wanting more, wanting another
Waiting most of my life!
I guess it all depends
On the uberousness of the wife

Poetry by Brian Mullins

coxcomb

Do you look into my eyes?
And see the same as me?
Or do you glance on past,
and see what you want to see.

Promises made, and promises broken,
Life goes on without a flinch.
Oft remembering what was our token,
But forgiveness is a cinch.

So on we go, fooling one another.
Going through and through...
So the question goes to answer
Am I the coxcomb or are you?

Authentic Perplexity

darkness

*In the darkness of youth
we writhe and grind
breaking ourselves
on the coldness of freedom*

*Knowing at a glance
but forgiving with frustration
do I dare confront
or only deny*

*My heart she wrenched
and smashed as well
burning my soul
condemning to hell*

*Death my option
numbness my desire
forgive her I cannot
do I dare try*

*Out of darkness came peace
and love divine
a red haired Saviour
to comfort and cherish*

*To this I do cling
a new light in life
the mother of my child
my newfound wife*

Poetry by Brian Mullins

desire

Glimmering light
seeded in darkness
pulsing, yearning for release

Pent up and pressured
building towards the top
releasing in climax

Do you see me?
Hidden beneath
golden waves of sorrow

Can you feel
the urge to complete
held back by past failures

I seek to finish all
a jigsaw puzzle
missing a corner

Holding back
A stile of my
life to yours

Authentic Perplexity

Pressing issues
falling behind
left over masonry

Moving on
a celestial event
timed by a stone

Poetry by Brian Mullins

random thoughts

Silence,
sought but not found.
Aspirating on freedom,
constrained by laughter.

Release me from myself,
For my mind knows not it's bounds.
I seek a flower, in a garden
where my heart has found contentment.

Random thoughts of the past,
Filtered by hate and greed
Seeking way into life
Finding darkness and death.

I am happy here,
nothing can change this fact.
I do not want to be again
Fondness of past redeems.

Hurt and pain caused by innocuousness
Fleeting harms healing breaks.
Mind swirling and confusing
Light of darkness one desire.

Authentic Perplexity

Love affairs gone awry
Plots and evils on the plumb
Future filled with love
Past filled with falsehood

Poetry by Brian Mullins

Brian Mullins is a father of four, author, poet, and artist. He is currently enrolled at the New York Institute of Photography and spends his time studying, raising and nurturing his children, and trying to be the best father he can. His loving wife Julie is as supportive as she can be, and is very understanding of his craft.

You can view more of his work online and contact him at his Myspace web presence, or via his Yahoo page. He also has a page setup with more of his artwork at the following locations:

http://www.myspace.com/authentic__perplexity
http://www.authenticperplexity.com
http://www.db.com/brian__mullins

email: zantocon@yahoo.com

He is currently working on his second book, "Musings in the Night" which is a look more into the darker and steamier side of his dreams.

Also visit his Lulu Storefront at:
http://stores.lulu.com/zantocon

www.ingramcontent.com/pod-product-compliance
Lightning Source LLC
Chambersburg PA
CBHW031623160426
43196CB00006B/259